DATE LOANED

DATE DUE

29 Jan '57 JO

22 Oct '59 AF

3 Dec '59 MT

11 Apr '60 KS
25 Dec '60 FS

23 Jun '62 TB
1 Aug '63 JG

22 Aug '63 MP

27 Apr '61 VW
4 Sep '64 R

31 J 1970 J

2 Aug '61 FS
18 MAR 1970 A

30 1970 K

R/ MV 2 MA 1973 D AR

THE REVOLUTIONARY MOVEMENT
IN FRANCE

THE REVOLUTIONARY MOVEMENT IN FRANCE

1815-71

by
JOHN PLAMENATZ
Fellow of Nuffield College, Oxford

1724

LONGMANS, GREEN AND CO
LONDON ❖ NEW YORK ❖ TORONTO

LONGMANS, GREEN AND CO LTD
6 & 7 CLIFFORD STREET LONDON WI
ALSO AT MELBOURNE AND CAPE TOWN

LONGMANS, GREEN AND CO INC
55 FIFTH AVENUE NEW YORK 3

LONGMANS, GREEN AND CO
215 VICTORIA STREET TORONTO I

ORIENT LONGMANS LTD
BOMBAY CALCUTTA MADRAS

First published 1952

PRINTED IN GREAT BRITAIN
BY WESTERN PRINTING SERVICES LTD., BRISTOL

PREFACE

I have to thank my wife, who has read the manu-
script of this book very carefully, for corrections of
grammar and style more numerous than I care to
remember. I have also to thank my uncle, M.
Pierre Matanovitch, for his valuable criticisms,
which have enabled me to avoid several mistakes,
especially in what I say about the church. I am still
uneasily aware that prejudices, difficult for anyone
educated in a Protestant country to discover and
allow for, may have warped my judgment.

J.P.

December, 1950

v

CONTENTS

CONTENTS

INTRODUCTION

I CANNOT call this book an historical essay, for it is less a commentary on events than an account of them. On the other hand, it is not the product of meticulous research; it brings to light no new facts and relies entirely on the discoveries of other people, on the many books written about the subject by French historians. But, whereas Englishmen who read history to enjoy it can nowadays discover easily enough—if only they have the time and thought to spare for an undertaking that can never be small—what happened in France during the great revolution, and even what followed from Thermidor until Napoleon's second fall, the facts collected and the theories made by historians about the radical and revolutionary movement of the nineteenth century lie scattered through the pages of a hundred books. Some of these books are excellent, and many of them easy to read. But they either discuss only a small part of my subject, or other subjects as well, or else are so strongly prejudiced as to mislead anyone who has not read other accounts of the matter. Not that I wish to condemn prejudice; though it blinds men when they look in some directions, it sharpens their vision when they look in others. Besides, it is usually natives who have the strongest prejudices, and it is also natives who understand their own countries best. The opinions about France of a prejudiced and intelligent Frenchman are often worth more than the opinions of a foreigner, however learned, patient and well-meaning he may be. Impartiality is not understanding; and we should always be conscious of this truth when we dabble in the history of another country. But impartiality is a virtue possible to the foreigner, and it has its good effects.

I have tried in this book to be lucid, exact and comprehensive, to put as much into it as I could without placing too great a burden on a small frame. I have had a complicated story to tell and I have wanted to leave out nothing essential to it. I have

therefore had, perforce, to be simple, because this is the economy
the historian can practise at least cost to his readers. What
sacrifice it involves is mostly his, for he must say his say without
the qualifications required, if not by wisdom, then at least by
prudence. He must sometimes speak with the assurance of the
novelist, of the man whose world exists only because he perceives
it.

I have not discussed in this book what some historians call the
"underlying causes" of revolution. I have tried to avoid the great
error of the Marxists, which is to search hard for the causes of
things before they have looked carefully at the things themselves.
They know, so they think, what revolutions are, and they also
know what kind of events their causes must be. This knowledge
they acquire not from history but from philosophy; and their task
as historians is to discover not what happened but what must have
happened. Their whole conception of history is false; it assumes
that the activities recorded by the historian can be divided into so
many categories, of which one is "fundamental" in relation to the
others. It is a gratuitous assumption because there is no evidence
of its truth; and it is also dangerous, because those who make it
look only for the evidence they want to find. Few contemporaries
looked more closely at the events this book describes than Karl
Marx; and he, if ever there was one, was a shrewd observer. But
he had the misfortune to provide himself, when still a young man,
with a philosophy that made it for ever impossible for him to
understand the course of events in France, the country that he
himself called revolutionary *par excellence*. And yet it is his
reactions to those events which have given the communists a
great part of their political theory, expounded in such pamphlets
as *The Communist Manifesto*, *The Eighteenth Brumaire of Louis
Bonaparte* and *The Civil War in France*. Marx, indeed, (for a man's
philosophy merely obstructs and does not destroy his intelligence)
noticed and recorded many facts that are inconsistent with his
theories; but when he drew his more general conclusions he
either forgot them or else was blind to their significance. He
thought that France was becoming more revolutionary as the
century progressed; and he mistook the Paris Commune for the
first battle in a new war between the proletariat and the bourgeoisie. He spoke contemptuously of Louis Blanc and Proudhon

and he never understood why it was that the French workers listened to them. There did at last come a time, after my period ends, when the French socialist movement became Marxist; but by then it had ceased to be revolutionary.

Nowhere else in the world has there been a series of revolutions to compare with the French ones of 1789 to 1871. The first and greatest of them was perhaps the least expected, the least controlled and the least doctrinaire; men's minds were prepared for it in the negative sense that philosophy had destroyed many of the beliefs and loyalties on which the old order rested, but there was no theory of government and society to guide the revolutionaries of 1789 to 1794; there were only the abstract principles of the rights of man. The writings of Voltaire, the Encyclopædists and Rousseau were among the important causes of the revolution, but they none of them—not even the *Social Contract*—provided the revolutionaries with a theory they could apply to the problems caused by the disintegration of the old France. If ever a political society existed that looked like a copy (though a very imperfect one) of the ideal state described by Rousseau, it was not the revolutionary France of the Jacobins but the Paris Commune of 1871. The Commune was a small political society, simple, equalitarian and democratic; it respected property, made provision for the poor, disliked the wealthy, mistrusted all authority not directly responsible to the people, and was never dominated by any organised party or any one faction. But the Communards were not disciples of Rousseau; if they took their doctrines from anyone, it was from Proudhon.

The revolution of 1830 was as little doctrinaire as the great one, but it was much better controlled. The republicans got less from it than they wanted but not much less than they expected, while the liberals were able to bring it to a halt just where it suited them. The revolution of 1848 was a greater and more complicated event; there were already several doctrines at large and also enthusiasts anxious to give effect to them. But nobody got what he wanted, except Louis Napoleon who only wanted power. The most pathetic and terrible of these revolutions was the last, for with a little good will and good sense it could easily have been avoided. There was no need for twenty thousand Frenchmen to die in Paris in 1871.

Historians sometimes speak of revolutions that failed and others that succeeded. The first French revolution was, they say, successful; so, too, the second; but not the third, and not the Commune. It is a mistake to pass such judgments as these; revolutions merely happen, they neither fail nor succeed. They are not persons and have no purposes. They are made by men or groups of men, whose purposes are not only different but always changing; they have their causes and their effects; they often greatly alter the societies in which they happen; but to speak of their failure or success is to make one or other of two assumptions, neither of which is true: that revolutions are made by some group or class of men who know what they want and act in consequence; or else that revolutions have an historical function, which is to propel society more quickly than it ordinarily moves along some predestined course. These assumptions are themselves legends created by the long series of French revolutions; and like other legends they, too, have affected the course of history.

If we wish to understand revolutions, we must take care never to forget the correct sequence of events in time. The social historian and the historian of ideas describe changes, reforms, inventions and theories whose influence is difficult to assess and extends over the years. So long only as we know within a year or two when these things happened, we can understand their significance, the influence of each of them on the society they belong to. The historian can discuss them separately, relying on his readers not to forget the whole of which they are only the parts. But when a revolution is described, nothing matters more than that the reader should know exactly what happened, where, how and when. If he does not know that one event came before another, he may miss the significance of both. In times of revolution men are affected by sudden fears and hopes; they make plans, change them quickly, and as quickly abandon them; the relative strengths of rival groups are never for long the same; opportunities come and go, often unseen; leaders act too early or else too late, and seldom at the best moment; they make their calculations, which are mostly wrong but not therefore unimportant, for they, too, may lead to actions that change the course of history. Revolutions are rightly called dramatic, not because they are violent, but because they have a certain unity about them, moving quickly from scene to scene, from a beginning to an end. In times of revolution, men excite and harry one another, and by so doing create a course of events that seems to sweep them along in spite of themselves; they become the victims of their own emotions and their own schemes. A revolution is not so much to be interpreted as to be told; and to be intelligible, it must be told in sufficient detail and in the proper order.

But a revolutionary movement is not a revolution; between the short revolutionary periods that seem so much longer than they actually were, there were the years of peace, years of restlessness or of apathy, of open opposition or of secret resistance. What was the revolutionary movement, and how did it affect the French revolutions of the nineteenth century?

By the revolutionary movement, I mean the activities of all the groups that wanted to destroy the monarchy, whether Bourbon or Bonapartist, in France. All these groups were not revolutionary; indeed, only a few of them were so, and they were the least popular. Yet they were all opponents of the régimes that only some of them destroyed; they all welcomed the revolutions after they had begun (with the single exception of the Commune); they all tried to control their courses, and they all contributed to make them possible. They were the spiritual posterity of the great revolution, which was, in one or another of its phases, the example and inspiration of them all. Even though they refrained from violence (which they mostly did), even though they some-times condemned it in the present, or for the future, they always praised or excused the great revolution and adhered to some of the principles proclaimed while it lasted. Their France was the France created by that revolution, and their task (as they saw it) to complete what it had begun. These groups did not like each other and their quarrels sometimes led to civil war; but for the greater part of our period they were, whether they liked it or not, allies. Again and again, during the fifty years before the final establishment of the republic, circumstances brought them together; and that republic was the product of their endeavours, their resistance, their revolutions, and even of their quarrels. They did what the great revolutionaries failed to do; they made France republican and they made her democratic. Had they not acted as they did, the revolutions (whether they intended them or not) would never have happened; and had they not happened, these groups would never have had their opportunities to make France, not only in name but in fact, what she has been ever since 1870—a democratic republic. That is why, in spite of all the differences between them, in spite of the fears, prudence and regrets of the moderates among them (who were always the great majority), their activities must all be included in the revolutionary movement. It was not until after 1870 that the differences between them counted for more than their common hostility to the friends of privilege, authoritarian government and the church.

Chapter One

THE GREAT REVOLUTION

I. REPUBLICANISM IN FRANCE

THE movement I call revolutionary might also be called republican; and, indeed, many Frenchmen have called it so. But this book is written for Englishmen, who think of republicanism as mere opposition to monarchy. The republican movement in nineteenth century France was much more than that; it was radical and also partly socialist, and above all it was revolutionary in a double sense; it was inspired by a great revolution and made three lesser ones. It is the movement that made France politically what she is to-day: a liberal and socialist democracy closer to England than she has ever been before.

It has been said that to be a republican in France is to accept the principles of the French Revolution, the first and great revolution of 1789 to 1794. But this revolution passed through many stages, until at last, in 1794, most people who would willingly have called themselves revolutionaries in 1789 hated and feared the new rulers of France more than they had ever done her kings. Modern France has never been divided into two broad classes of people: those who accepted the great revolution and those who condemned it. There have, of course, been people who condemned it, who thought that France in 1789 took the first step on the long road to decay and anarchy. For a few years, in the reign of Charles X, it seemed that these people might become the sole rulers of France. But it needed only the gentlest of French revolutions to send them scuttling out of the country. The really formidable enemies of the republicans in France were not the Legitimists, but the Orleanists and Bonapartists, themselves also, though in a different sense, heirs of the great revolution. The restorations of 1814 and 1815 restored nothing except the monarchy; nor did they destroy anything created by the revolution that had not already been destroyed by the Directory and by Bonaparte. More formidable even than the Orleanists and Bonapartists was the church, the greatest of all the enemies of republicanism. The church, you may say, was a survival from the *ancien régime*. She most certainly was so, but a survival not only from the old monarchy as it had developed under the successors of Henry IV; she owed even more to régimes much older than the absolute government of the Bourbons. Though the church was sometimes on good terms with the Legitimists, she had no strong preference for them. She had perhaps a special sympathy for them as for persons who had also greatly suffered during the Terror. The church was strong, and yet not strong enough to do without powerful allies. The Legitimists were never really powerful and only sometimes looked as if they were so.

Besides, the church, the most formidable enemy of the republicans, was also, in one sense, the creation, though not exactly the heir, of the great revolution. She was of course always the same church, preaching the same doctrines and having the same mission on earth. But she was a church purified, disciplined and centralised. The authority of bishops over the lower clergy, and of the Pope over the bishops was much greater than it had been before 1789. Gallicanism was not dead but it was slowly dying. Morally and politically, the Catholic Church in France was stronger in the nineteenth than she had been in the eighteenth century; she was also much more independent, if not of Rome, then of Paris. In the eighteenth century, the monarchy and the church, both of them corrupt, badly organised and politically indifferent, scarcely understanding the dangers that threatened France and themselves, leant heavily against each other. They were not so much allies, having common purposes and acting together by agreement, as old companions who had no ambition except to survive and who felt too weak to stand without each other's support. But the revolution had given new strength to the old church; it had reconciled the higher and the lower clergy by persecuting them both and by destroying the temporal privileges of the former. The first republic had made war on the church; the control of the state had passed into the hands of the enemies of religion. The French church, which had once sought the support of the state against what she considered the excessive claims of the papacy, had learned that independence of Rome can only be had at the cost of a much greater and more dangerous dependence on the secular power. The revolution made the church what she had ceased to be in the eighteenth century, an active and intelligent political force, choosing her allies according to the needs of the moment yet always faithful to her mission on earth. That mission was to maintain religion, and therefore to preserve and, if possible, to increase whatever control the church had over education. The French church in the nineteenth century never sought political power for herself; she had no ambition to rule the state, either openly or secretly. But she fought hard to prevent the domination of the state by the enemies of religion. She was therefore politically active, since the enemies of religion, or rather of the Catholic Church, sought political power. These enemies were, of course, the republicans.

Who then were the republicans? Broadly speaking, they were the heirs of the Convention and of the Commune, of the first Commune, the revolutionary municipal assembly which, with the help of the Jacobins, really destroyed the old monarchy in France. The Convention and the Commune included many different sorts of people, some of them very timid and respectable souls. They quarrelled with each other much more than they agreed. But in 1792 they had this in common: they were against the monarchy, they were hostile to the church, and they believed that the victory of reaction could only be prevented by inciting the people against the throne and all its supporters. In 1789 almost everyone who had political opinions had wanted great changes; in 1792 the minority of Frenchmen actively interested in politics were divided into two groups, of which one was much larger than the other. The larger group were afraid that the revolution had got out of hand; they feared disorder and war, and they thought that only the monarchy could save them from either. The smaller group, the Jacobins and their allies, feared reaction and distrusted the king. To prevent reaction they were prepared to use the mobs of Paris and of some of the other large towns. These mobs were a mere untidy handful of the French people, but those who sought their alliance, those who were not afraid to use them, were not therefore reluctant to call themselves democrats. The Jacobins of 1792, the true ancestors of the French republicans, were anti-clericals and democrats. Many of them, more especially the Girondins, later regretted their behaviour in that year. They too, in their turn, were to be denounced as counter-revolutionaries and enemies of the republic, but in 1792 they were both revolutionaries and republicans.

Now, the Jacobins of 1792 and their allies in Paris and some of the other large towns, though they were so small a minority of Frenchmen, were never, once the monarchy was overthrown, to act together as friends. The history of the revolution from August 10th, 1792 until the *coup d'état* of the 9th Thermidor (July 27th, 1794) is the history of quarrels to the death between republicans and of the opportunities created by these quarrels for enemies of the revolution. We must, if we are to distinguish between the various brands of republicanism that flourished in the nineteenth century, understand these quarrels. The republicans, like everyone else, evolved during that century, taking up attitudes and theories unheard of under the first republic. But the republicans always looked back to the first revolution as to the great example and inspiration of their lives. It was the only past event with which they were almost as familiar as with the France they lived in. It was the creator of the modern society whose government it was their ambition to control. Of the much older France, from which their society was as truly descended as from the great revolution, they knew all too little. In their eyes, what had happened in France before 1789 was almost pre-history.

The republicans were, in a quite peculiar sense, the children of the great revolution, especially of the last phase of that revolution. The other principal actors on the French political stage during the nineteenth century, the Bonapartists, the Orleanists, and even the church (as a political agent) were also, if you like, creatures of the revolution. If it had not been for the revolution, neither Bonapartists nor Orleanists would have existed; and the political behaviour of the church would have been quite different. But these other groups, though the revolution made them what they were, were never, as were the republicans, the apologists of the revolution. They had not ruled France at the height of the revolution. They were not the friends, but the victims, enemies or successors of the Convention, the Jacobin Club and the Com-

mune. That is why there is no understanding French republicanism unless you know what happened in France during the last
two years of the revolution, the twenty-three months when
France was governed by the Convention, the Club and the Paris
Commune. And there is no understanding French socialism
either, except on the same terms, for that socialism was the natural
product of the republicans' interest in the welfare of their most
effective allies, the poor. Not all French socialists were republicans. Some of the socialist philosophers, for instance Saint-
Simon and Fourier, despised and ignored all political movements
indifferently. But I am not speaking of socialist theories; I am
speaking of French socialism as a political and social force. As
such it is an integral part of the republican movement, as politically radical and as much inclined to revolution. It is, therefore,
just as much as any other part of the movement, the heir of the
Convention, the Clubs and the Commune.

Before I attempt a short but very necessary account of what
happened in France between August 1792 and July 1794, I must
say just one thing more to make my general purpose more
intelligible. What I shall be trying to do is to describe, not the
evolution of political theories, but the behaviour of political
movements. Of course, in an old and complex society, where
literature and philosophy are held in the highest esteem, there
are no important political movements without their attendant
theories. But the influence of political theory on political conduct, important and undeniable though it is, is always indirect
and difficult to calculate. Theories must be reduced to slogans
before they can inspire conduct, and only small parts of them can
be so reduced. They must not only be reduced to the merest
fragments of themselves; they must also, if they are to be useful
in practice, be distorted and mixed up with fragments taken from
other systems. It would, I think, be a mistake to introduce long
accounts of socialist theories into what is intended to be a history
not of ideas but of political movements.

II. THE LEGACY OF THE FIRST REVOLUTION

Most of the permanent achievements of the great revolution
were the work of men who were monarchists. The institutions

they destroyed were never again established. It was they who abolished the last remnants of feudalism, who substituted the departments for the old provinces of France, who first imposed taxes on the privileged, who put an end to the sale of offices and to the lavish spending of public money for private purposes. It was they, too, who confiscated the property of the church, not from hostility to religion but because France was threatened with bankruptcy. The need to provide regular incomes for a clergy now deprived of revenues from church lands obliged them to make a statute for the church, the famous Civil Constitution of the Clergy. This statute was, on the whole, well received by the French clergy. The bishops were anxious that the Pope should sanction it. What was lost was, they thought, irretrievably lost, and it was now a question of making the best terms possible with the state. The lower clergy, with not many exceptions, were reconciled to a revolution which proposed almost to double their pitiful salaries. If the Pope had done what the French Church mostly wished him to do, one of the greatest disasters of the revolutionary period might have been avoided. But the Pope, influenced by the *émigrés* and the Catholic powers, refused. His refusal meant that most of the bishops and the lower clergy felt themselves obliged, as a matter of conscience, to refuse the oath required by the state. The Assembly did nothing to exasperate the church. Where other priests could not be found to take over, the non-jurors continued to serve. Where they were deprived of their cures, a pension was granted them. The Assembly had no wish to make an enemy of a church, which had, during the first phase of the revolution, proved herself more accommodating and reasonable than the old nobility. Besides, the French were still very strongly attached to their church. The philosophers had no influence outside the narrow circles of the educated; and there was certainly more unbelief among the bishops than among the peasants and urban poor. But the breach between the revolution and the church, though neither the clergy nor the Assembly were anxious to widen it, was none the less there. Should more extreme revolutionaries, men unwilling to turn a blind eye to uncomfortable facts, gain control of the state, a bitter conflict was inevitable.

The permanent achievements of the revolution were all the

work of the Constituent Assembly, the most freely chosen and widely representative of all the assemblies elected in France before 1848. The Constituent Assembly was always monarchist. Nothing can prove this so well as its reaction to the flight to Varennes. The king's intention had been to flee the country and to place himself under the protection of his brother-in-law, the Emperor. He was arrested, together with the queen, but he was neither deposed nor suspended. The Assembly decided to behave as if nothing had happened, as if the king had not made manifest his hostility to the revolution. The Assembly and the government pretended that the king had been kidnapped. If they were to depose him, they did not know where to find his successor. The king's brothers were *émigrés*, declared enemies of the new France. His cousin, the Duke of Orleans, was an extreme radical and nowhere popular except among his friends. The proclamation of a republic would, so thought the deputies, be an even worse mistake; it would give some demagogue or ambitious general (perhaps Lafayette) the chance to become a dictator. The safest régime, and therefore the best, was a conservative parliamentary monarchy and a decentralised administration. This was the régime the Constituent Assembly sought to establish. It had itself been chosen by the immense majority of adult Frenchmen, but it saw to it that a much smaller electorate should choose its successor. The first French Constitution, made by the Constituent Assembly, gave just over four million men the vote out of a population of twenty-six millions. Or in other words, of France's seven million families, the three million poorest were disfranchised.

By the autumn of 1791, when the Legislative Assembly took over from the Constituent, most Frenchmen thought the revolution had gone far enough, or else were indifferent to it or hostile. How then did it come about that the republicans, a small minority, became within ten months the masters of France?

The answer is simple: intrigue, inflation, Paris and war. The conservatives—and by conservatives I mean all those people, the great majority of Frenchmen not indifferent to politics, who accepted the revolution and the monarchy but now wanted to put a stop to the former and a limit to the latter—were divided, irresolute and without effective instruments of coercion. The conservatives could never have won their early victories against the court without the assistance of the Paris mob. It was the mob that in July 1789 had taken the Bastille, and in October of the same year had marched to Versailles and forced court and assembly to move to Paris. These easy and astonishing victories had made the revolution possible because they had shown that the king could not or at least dared not rely on the army. But the conservatives did not and had never controlled the mob. Nor could they all place the same reliance on the National Guard, created by the middle classes to protect themselves and their property from the mob. For though the National Guard was a bourgeois affair, it was never the instrument of either the Constituent or the Legislative Assembly. At its head in Paris was Lafayette, always suspected by many conservatives of aiming at the dictatorship. Besides, neither the Constituent nor the Legislative Assembly was a disciplined body. The ministers were responsible to the king, and there was no government, no front bench in either Assembly to give a lead to the deputies. The king intrigued against his ministers or through them against both Assemblies. The Assemblies distrusted the king and yet thought France could not do without a monarchy. The king, who had done violence to his conscience by accepting the Civil Constitution of the clergy, had no intention of making a permanent settlement with the revolutionaries, however conservative they might be. He was in touch with the émigrés, with the courts of Vienna and Berlin, and even with the clubs in Paris, whose violence might, he hoped, serve him against the Assembly and against Lafayette. The conservatives were no doubt the majority, but they were an irritated, suspicious and unorganised majority. They wanted to save the monarchy, but the court was determined to ruin them.

Worse even than their intrigues and confusion were the effects of inflation. Against the lands confiscated from the church and from the émigrés, certificates or assignats had been issued. The security against them was excellent, for it was much of the best land in France. But since sales of land take time, the assignats, although they were not legal tender, changed hands frequently before any land was sold. From the first, because of rumours of difficulties in connexion with the sale of land, the assignats were at a discount. And in any case they created inflation, for they were money put into circulation for many months and even years before the property against which they were issued was sold. By the end of April 1792, about 2,500 millions' worth of *assignats* had been issued and only just under 400 millions' worth had been called in, though confiscated property to several times that value had already been sold. Eventually, of course, all the confiscated property was sold, and every purchaser of it, whether bourgeois or peasant, became a firm supporter of the revolution or, rather, of the first, conservative phase of the revolution. But this did not prevent the evils of inflation. On the contrary, it enabled the extreme republicans to exploit these evils all the more effectively, because the purchasers and would-be purchasers of confiscated property were even more frightened of reaction than of continued revolution. It is this fact, indeed, that, perhaps more than any other, distinguishes the first from all later French revolutions: it was the only revolution when the middle class and the peasants feared reaction even more than radicalism. Meanwhile, the inflation exasperated the poor, especially the urban poor.

And then there was Paris. The conservatives were weak in Paris, the huge metropolis where the effects of inflation were felt more acutely than elsewhere. In Paris it was the clubs and the municipal authorities that were powerful. The most important of these clubs, a club originally formed by the Breton deputies at Versailles, moved to Paris with the king and the Assembly in October 1789. It held its meetings in the library of the Jacobin monastery in the Rue St. Honoré. By the end of 1790 it had a thousand members and was in correspondence with similar clubs in all the large provincial towns. At first there were many conservatives in the Jacobin Club, but by the end of 1791 its conservative members, finding its atmosphere less and less congenial, had deserted it. The Jacobin Club, with its affiliated societies in the rest of France, was never a political party. It had no recognised leaders, but was dominated now by one man and now by another. It had no settled principles and no programme. But it was continually active, in close touch with the municipal authorities and with all the radical minorities in the provinces. It was the nearest thing in France to an organised and centralised political organisation, and from 1791 onwards it was strongly republican.

There were other clubs, some more extreme than the Jacobins, but none that had the same power.

The first French Constitution, the one made by the conservative and monarchist Constituent Assembly, had created strong local governments all over France. Paris had had a powerful municipal council and 48 sectional councils (one for each section into which the capital had been divided) ever since June 1790. These councils, especially the sectional ones, had ever since been in the closest touch with the radical clubs. The revolutionary Commune did not come into existence until the night of August 9th–10th, 1792, but already for two years before the insurrection that was to destroy the monarchy, Paris, the chief victim of the inflation, had been steadily going radical.

I have tried to show how intrigue, inflation and the special position of Paris strengthened the republicans. What gave them their first opportunity was the war, declared by France against the Emperor in April 1792. With a little good will the war could easily have been avoided, because the European monarchs had no serious intention of wasting money and men to save the king of France. It was the French who provoked the war, not for the sake of conquest (for this ambition was not important until after the first victories had stimulated it) but because various political groups thought they could use it to become masters of France. The court thought that France, now almost in a state of anarchy, would be easily defeated and the royal power restored; Lafayette hoped that as a victorious general he would find it more easy to control the Assembly and frighten the clubs; while the majority of the republicans wanted war because they attributed the disturbances and the inflation that were wasting the energies of France to the intrigues of the *émigrés* and the powers. So France, in 1792 as in 1870, plunged recklessly into a war for which she was badly prepared; and in both cases the result was the establishment of a republic to which Paris alone was unequivocally loyal.

When several powerful groups in a country at war are more interested in defeating their domestic rivals than in victory over the enemy, there is bound to be treachery. And where there is treachery there are even more accusations of treachery. The court was in touch with the enemy from the beginning, and a few months later Lafayette, despairing of leading the demoralised army to victory, followed the royal example. Lafayette also decided to march on Paris and to put down the clubs. When on August 8th, 1792, the Legislative Assembly absolved Lafayette of the charges brought against him, the clubs and the Parisians decided to take action. On the night of August 9th–10th, the Parisian sections elected commissioners who constituted themselves a revolutionary Commune, or municipal assembly, in the Town Hall. It was this Commune and the Jacobin Club that organised the insurrection of August 10th, which put an end to the monarchy.

August 10th, 1792, is the day that separates the first, conservative phase of the revolution from the second and republican one. It also marks the victory of the Commune and the clubs over the Assembly. There had been insurrections before August 10th, but they had been directed against the royal power, whose limitation was from the beginning recognised as the prime object of revolutionary endeavour. But now Paris had defied and forced obedience on an Assembly itself created by the first revolutionary constitution. This Assembly, under pressure from the clubs and the Commune, confirmed the latter in its usurped authority; it also agreed to suspend the king and to order the immediate election of a new legislature, which was to prepare another constitution for France. The republicans excused their action, saying they had saved the revolution from its enemies. They had carried out their insurrection in the name of the people, but the fact remains that they used violence against the only body in France that could claim to be in any way representative of the people. Thus was created one of the oldest of European revolutionary traditions: that of the organised minority enforcing the "will of the people" against their elected representatives.

All the republicans had approved the insurrection of August 10th but not all had an equal hand in preparing it. The republicans, even before August 10th, had begun to divide into a more moderate and a more radical group. The moderates had favoured war; the radicals, with Robespierre and Marat at their head, had opposed it. The moderation of the moderates consisted chiefly in this, that they were wealthier, stronger in the provinces and weaker in Paris than the radicals. But they were just as hostile to monarchy and just as much afraid of a military dictatorship as the followers of Robespierre and Marat. They were also, at least before August 10th, just as ready to resort to force when they thought they could use it profitably. They had themselves staged an insurrection on June 20th, but it had failed. Fear of the court and of Lafayette bound them close to the radicals until the immediate danger of reaction was over, that is, until the insurrection of August 10th had succeeded. But once it had succeeded, they soon realised how much more the radicals stood to gain by it than they did themselves. As they were stronger in the Assembly than the radicals and had much less influence with the Commune and the sections, they took up the defence of the Assembly against the Parisians.

This was how the first split between the republicans began. They did not at first quarrel over policy, nor did they ever come to consider themselves as representing different classes and interests. But as the quarrel developed, it insensibly changed character. The moderates, especially when they began to lose power, became more moderate and more inclined to come to terms with the conservatives; while the radicals, resorting to terror and finding that no one supported them except the more desperate poor, became inevitably more radical. That is why some historians have been able plausibly to say that nothing divided the Girondins from the Mountain except rivalry for power; while others, equally plausibly, have argued that they represented different classes of the community. As the Girondins moved to the right and the Montagnards to the left, the struggle between them, originally a dispute between rival republican groups nearly all of whose members belonged to the Jacobin Club, became a social war of the propertied against the propertyless, of the provinces against Paris and of the clubs and Commune against the third revolutionary assembly, the Convention.

I shall not follow the development of this struggle in any detail but I must say something about it. A conflict of the same kind between republicans was to break out during two subsequent French revolutions—those of 1848 and 1871. The peculiarity of the first revolution is that it was the only occasion when the radicals succeeded in becoming masters not only of Paris but of France. The first example of a conflict three times repeated in

French history is clearly a phenomenon of the greatest importance to my subject.

One of the first consequences of the ascendancy of the Commune and of the Paris sections was the massacre in early September of political prisoners in the capital and also, though the victims were fewer, in some of the provincial towns. The Commune and the sections were doing their best to organise resistance in Paris against the advancing Prussians; they were determined, if they should have to march out against the enemy, to leave no traitors behind. From eleven to fourteen hundred people were put to death in Paris alone. One of the first acts of the republicans was therefore to show that they were prepared to shed the blood of their enemies recklessly. And at the same time, they began an offensive against the priests. Hitherto the revolution had not deliberately interfered with the church except with the approval of the great majority of the clergy. If it had already provoked a breach between church and state, this was only because the Pope's intransigence had obliged the great majority of the clergy to condemn what they had originally been willing to approve, or at least to tolerate. But now the republicans wilfully attacked the clergy, whose influence at the coming elections for the Convention they greatly feared. The decree of August 26th ordered non-juring (or, as the French put it, refractory) priests to leave France within fifteen days. Perhaps 25,000 priests left the country, and many thousands more went into hiding. It had not taken the republicans long to prove that the new revolutionary rulers of France were quite different from the old. Here was bloodshed on a scale unknown to France for many generations, and the persecution of priests whom most Frenchmen looked upon as the only true representatives of their church.

In the elections for the Convention every adult Frenchman had the right to vote. And yet they were the most poorly attended of the three elections of the first revolution. Fewer people voted than in either 1791 or 1789. Except in Paris and some other towns the men of property got their way undisputed. All French historians agree that the deputies to the Convention were elected by a resolute minority. And only a minority of these deputies, themselves elected by a minority of Frenchmen, were supporters of Robespierre and the men of August 10th.

The first eight months of the Convention, which met on September 21st, 1792, were taken up by a bitter struggle for power between the republicans who had made the insurrection of August 10th and the republicans who had been obliged to accept its consequences. The former, known to history as the Mountain, were led by Robespierre and Marat; the latter, the Girondins, were led by a group of deputies, some of whom came from Paris but most of them from the south, especially the valley of the Gironde. The Girondins had done better in the elections than the Mountain, though it had been Robespierre and the Commune who had insisted on their being held. The Mountain could not therefore refuse to accept the verdict of the people. The insurrectionary Commune, established on the eve of August 10th, allowed itself to be dissolved after the elections and before the Convention met; and soon after there came news of Valmy and then of other victories against the enemy. The panic fear and suspicion that had made possible both the insurrection of August 10th and the September massacres had now subsided. It looked as if the Girondins were alone to profit from the insurrection made by their rivals. They were able to exploit the resentment felt against the Parisians for their presumptuous violence and the shame occasioned by the September massacres. The Girondins were fast becoming what the moderate republicans were to be in all later French revolutions: the champions of provincial France against the audacities and brutalities of Paris, the defenders of law against violence, the defenders of property against the demagogues. To mark their new attitude to the Mountain, the Girondins in October 1792 left the Jacobin Club. They might have disputed control of it with the Mountain but they preferred to abandon it. They called upon the provincial clubs to break affiliation with the Jacobins, but only a few, like those at Marseilles and Lyon, responded. The Girondins never established a club or a system of clubs of their own. They preferred to be respectable, to meet in drawing rooms and there to decide policy. In this way they lost what influence they had in Paris and yet failed to organise their supporters in the rest of France.

While France was victorious, the Girondins were strong. But in the spring of 1793 the tide turned against France, and in a few weeks all the conquests of the previous autumn and winter were lost. The early French victories had been due, above all, to the great numerical superiority of the French armies. The war, in spite of these difficulties, had been mismanaged. Desertions were frequent, the supply services poor, the generals obstructive and disobedient, and the old regular troops and new volunteer units on the worst of terms with each other. Defeat and invasion obliged the republic to raise new armies, and the attempt to recruit soldiers in the provinces where the republic was most unpopular led to revolt. On the top of all this, there came the treachery of Dumouriez, the favourite general of the Girondins.

Defeat, panic and treachery, this time with civil war added to them, again gave the radicals their opportunity. The Paris sections and the Jacobin Club staged the insurrection of May 31st, 1793, of which the prime movers were again Robespierre and Marat. For the second time, a French National Assembly was invaded by the mob; and the deputies were this time forced to sanction the arrest of twenty-nine of their members, the leaders of the Gironde. In the provinces the Girondins provoked insurrections against the new masters of Paris and of France, but they were poorly organised and could not dislodge their enemies from power. They did, for a time, capture Bordeaux, Lyon and several other towns, and they let the English into Toulon. Because they were fighting not only for power but for survival, they were unscrupulous. Where they could do so to advantage, they made common cause with the royalists and refractory priests, the "reactionaries" they had themselves denounced only a few months earlier.

The radicals ruled France from the beginning of June 1793 until the *coup d'état* of the 9th Thermidor (July 27th, 1794), which put an end to the Terror and to Robespierre. For fourteen months they were the rulers of France, unpopular, ruthless and triumph-ant. A fortnight after they came to power, about sixty of the eighty-three French departments were in more or less open revolt against them. France was again invaded and there seemed to be no troops in the country capable of resisting the invader. And yet within a year, the republic had triumphed over her domestic and foreign enemies, she had larger and better equipped armies than ever before and generals who could be trusted not to betray their country. If efficiency means harmonious co-operation and energy put to the best uses, it is clear that the first republic was never efficient. Rival groups disputed control of the Commune, the sections and the clubs with greater ferocity than ever. If the Convention was more or less docile, the committees through which the Mountain dominated it were never at peace. Indeed, Thermidor would have been impossible if some of the members of the Committee of Public Safety had not joined the conspiracy against Robespierre, the most powerful member of that committee. Robespierre himself was never a dictator. France, indeed, has never yet been at the mercy of doctrinaires. The members of the Committee of Public Safety were ardent patriots, true republicans, enemies of the rich and of the clergy whom they suspected of treachery to the republic. But they were otherwise just as much opportunists as Napoleon himself. In their temper and sympathies they differed widely from him, but their actions were just as little inspired by a general theory about the nature of human societies and governments. And it is this temper and these sympathies that constitute the radical republican tradition in nineteenth century France.

Because the Mountain knew that the provinces were hostile to them, they put their faith in Paris; because they could trust so few people and felt themselves surrounded by secret enemies and traitors, they resorted to terror; because the rich and the peasants profited from inflation, bought up scarce commodities and resented the regulation of prices and the control of distribution made necessary by the war, they felt that their truest friends were the poor, the men of no property who would starve if prices were not fixed and supplies ensured. In the end, the Mountain, conscious of their isolation and perhaps feeling that victory would soon make Terror inexcusable, conceived of a great transfer of property to the advantage of their friends. A decree passed at the end of February 1794 ordered the confiscation of the property of all enemies of the republic, that is to say, of all the political prisoners detained in France. Another decree ordered the communal authorities all over the country to prepare lists of poor people. As there were 300,000 political prisoners in France at that time, many of them rich, the transfer of property proposed was immense. There had, of course, been confiscations of property on a very great scale, even during the first, conservative, phase of the revolution. But this property, taken from the church and the *émigrés*, was sold to the highest bidder. Most of it was bought by the rich and a substantial amount by the peasants. It had been a transfer of property from some propertied men to others. It had been a purely financial and political measure, undertaken in the first instance to pay off part of the national debt and balance the budget. But the new proposed transfer was quite different in kind; it was intended to reduce inequality and to attach the poor to the new rulers of France. It was certainly not a socialist measure, for it was inspired by motives of political expediency, and yet it was a measure which, if it had been carried out, would have had the most important social consequences. And if it was not carried out, it was only because the 9th Thermidor happened just in time to prevent it.

The first French revolution, even in its second, republican phase, was always a bourgeois revolution. Not a single person who attained power or influence in France between 1789 and 1794 could be described as either a socialist or a communist. There were people who preached communism in France during the first revolution; they were more numerous and more listened to than they had been before 1789, but they were never formidable. Even the famous communist conspiracy of 1796, Babeuf's "Conspiration des Egaux," was not nearly so important as some historians have said it was. It was above all a protest against the corruption, luxury and indifference to the poor that had prevailed in France ever since Thermidor. The number of persons implicated in the conspiracy was small, and it is doubtful whether most of them knew what their leaders wanted. Babeuf's conspiracy gave birth to an important legend, but in itself it was not important.

The first French revolution was not socialist. It was not even proletarian at any stage of its development. True, the Paris mob played an important part, but the men who controlled and moved the mob were all bourgeois. The workers were the instruments of middle class radicals whose first object was certainly not the enfranchisement and enrichment of the proletariat. But though the workers were instruments, they were willing and even enthusiastic instruments. The radical republicans, the followers of Marat and Robespierre, had made an alliance with the workers,

C

especially with the workers of Paris. This alliance had been indispensable to their success. It had been made effective through the close co-operation of the Jacobin Club with the Commune and the sections, that is to say, with the municipal authorities elected by the workers. This was the alliance that had made possible the insurrections of August 10th and May 31st, that had enabled a small minority, whose power was centred in Paris, to dominate the whole of France and to defeat all enemies, domestic and foreign.

I have said that the first revolution was neither socialist nor proletarian. That is certainly true. But there is another truth equally important to remember. Lichtenberger has put it extremely well in his book on *Socialism and the French Revolution*. He says that in 1793 a new antagonism, that between the rich and the poor, replaced the old one between the privileged and the unprivileged. The radical republicans, the Montagnards, whose activities brought this change about, never thought of themselves as the enemies of property, but it was precisely in this character that they appeared to their victims.

Chapter Two

THE RESTORATION

WHAT sort of a country was France in 1814 and 1815, when the Bourbons were restored? Were there any republicans, democrats or radicals left there twenty years after the fall of Robespierre?

The French were perhaps never less interested in politics than at the end of the first Empire. The republic was a bad memory, and the Bourbons almost forgotten. Their really devoted adherents were mostly outside France, *émigré* nobles and refractory priests who had learned to love the old monarchy because its fall had been the occasion of their own sufferings. Even the allied monarchies that defeated France had forgotten the Bourbons. So much had happened since 1792 that Europe had never lived through twenty-two years that seemed longer. But the Bourbons had one great advantage. No one feared them. Feudalism had been so long abolished, the property confiscated during the first revolution so long in the possession of its new owners, the regicides so long unpunished, that it seemed to everyone that what had been done more than twenty crowded years ago could not now be undone. Napoleon was impossible because he was defeated, and the republic because the rich and the peasants were afraid of it. The Terror had immunised France against the republic, and more than one generation was needed for its effects to wear away.

The allies had no intention of forcing the Bourbons on France in 1814. It was only at his second restoration in 1815 that Louis XVIII returned to his capital in the wake of the invader. In 1814 it was a handful of Frenchmen, bankers, high officials and soldiers, who had made or increased their fortunes under Napoleon, who persuaded the allies that Louis XVIII should become King of France. They prepared demonstrations to prove to the allies that the Bourbons were still popular, and to dispel the Tsar's fear that their restoration would lead to another revolution and another war. The prime movers in this plot were men like Talleyrand, Fouché and the banker Lafitte. It was after a meeting with Lafitte that Marshal Marmont deserted the Emperor and forced his abdication at Fontainebleau. These rich and eminent men, soldiers, ministers, bankers and senators, felt no gratitude to Napoleon. He had made their fortunes but he had also hurt their vanity. He was a hard, rude and restless master. They now wanted peace and the opportunity to enjoy their great wealth; they also wanted a weak master who, unlike the Emperor, would have to share his power with them.

Louis XVIII, his return to the throne prepared by men who had served Napoleon, was not ungrateful. He granted a constitution to France, a very conservative constitution, but one quite liberal enough for the rich and ambitious men he wanted to reward. He was anxious not to lose the throne he had come by after so many years, and he thought the men who had deserted Napoleon his most useful allies. They were supple, experienced and reasonable; they had stayed in France and understood what that country had become in the last twenty-five years. If they thought his return possible and were disposed to help him, he would not inquire into the past nor make difficulties for them.

Unfortunately for Louis and his new friends, the king did not return alone. There came with him many thousands of exiles, noblemen and priests, victims of the revolution, who expected France to undo the injustices done to them. From the moment of their return their extravagant language and threats frightened everyone. They were almost the only people capable of rousing France from her apathy. But for them, the restoration might have been as quiet as it was easy, and Napoleon have remained in Elba dangerous to no one. The *émigrés* frightened the peasants and the middle class, the two great beneficiaries of the revolution. Napoleon took his chance, and was welcomed back again with enthusiasm only a few months after he had left unregretted by the great majority of Frenchmen. Their second exile exasperated the *émigrés*. After Waterloo, they organised a White Terror, and by means of it succeeded in winning the first parliamentary elections under the new constitution.

The political history of France during the restoration is merely the record of a struggle for power between two very small minorities, the *émigré* nobles and the clergy, on the one hand, against the upper middle class on the other. The former were known as the ultra-royalists and the latter as the liberals. The ultras accepted the parliamentary régime because the king had established it, but they asserted his right to withdraw whatever privileges he had granted. The liberals approved of parliamentary government as a matter of principle, and denied the king's right to abolish the constitution. This was supposed to be the great difference between the two parties; but as a matter of fact, because Louis XVIII distrusted the ultras and feared their folly, the liberals were sometimes better champions of the royal power than the royalists.

What were the reactions of the rest of France while these two small groups were playing the parliamentary game, whose rules neither very scrupulously respected? France was indifferent. Except when they feared for their land, the peasants took no interest in politics. It was not until much later in the century that the political activity of the peasants ceased to be occasional and negative. The peasants may, perhaps, have liked Napoleon; at least they had been very much aware of his existence and greatly impressed by him. Otherwise, their political reactions were governed by fear, and more specifically by two fears: that some part of their land might be taken from them to satisfy the returned *émigrés*, and that the republicans of Paris, the most godless, ruthless and bloodthirsty of men, might again rule France. Until 1848 they were untroubled by the latter fear, and with every year after 1815 the former grew fainter. The peasants from 1815 to 1848 tilled the soil, troubled no one and were themselves untroubled.

The lower middle class and the urban workers, the only true supporters of the republicans from 1792 to 1794, were also, for the time being, quiescent. The lesser bourgeoisie had, since 1794, fallen under the spell of Napoleon, but the Emperor had been too recently defeated for his sympathisers to be active. The workers were even more silent and inscrutable than the peasants. Very little had been heard of them since the fall of Robespierre. The authorities had never forgotten their part, auxiliary but indispensable, in the Terror. Napoleon's police had paid special attention to them, and his codes had discriminated against them. Real wages had fallen steadily for the last twenty years, and alone of all Frenchmen except the *émigrés*, their standard of living was much lower than it had been before 1789. They were a truly depressed class, and because Robespierre and the Mountain had befriended them, few people in France sympathised with them.

If republicanism were ever to become important in France, it must regain its hold on the classes and groups most ready to accept it during the first revolution. It must begin again where it had begun before; but this time progress might be more difficult. In 1792 there had been few republicans in France, but no one had yet learnt to fear and to hate them. In 1815 there were still fewer, and by those who remembered the Terror they were execrated.

The republicans made only a little progress from 1815 to 1830, but they made just enough to enable them to prevent a weak and foolish king, Charles X, from destroying the constitution and to scare him from the throne. All the political forces active in France for a generation after Napoleon's fall were weak. Nine-tenths of France was politically indifferent and socially conservative. It was not difficult to make a revolution, but it was unlikely that the revolution, once made, would greatly disturb the country. This, perhaps, was fortunate for the republicans, because after 1830 it made both revolution and themselves appear less dangerous and more respectable than before.

In 1815 the only republicans in France were a few old men, survivors from the Convention, the Commune and the Clubs who had not gone over to Napoleon and had therefore been unimportant for twenty years. These survivors from the great days, or from the days that were to appear great as soon as a republican legend was created, made their first converts among the students of the University of Paris. They passed on the tradition by word of mouth. It was in September 1818 that the Paris students formed their first republican association under cover of freemasonry. The founder of this association, or Freemasons' lodge called the *Friends of Truth*, was the student Bazard. The Paris students were therefore the first organised republicans in nineteenth-century France, and they were also revolutionaries. Less than two years after this lodge was formed, Bazard and his friends plotted an insurrection in which 600 armed students were to have taken part. The police got wind of the plot and it came to nothing; but it is significant that republicanism was scarcely reborn before it decided to resort to arms.

The students were not discouraged by the failure of their first plot. Two members of the *Friends of Truth* went to Naples to study the organisation of the *Carbonari*, at that time engaged in a successful revolution against the Neapolitan Bourbons. When they returned they founded, together with Bazard, the French *Charbonnerie*. This new association was not confined to students or republicans, but took in all opponents of the régime who were not afraid of a little conspiracy and violence.

The *Charbonnerie* spread rapidly, and it soon contained far more Bonapartists than republicans. Its members came mostly from the lower middle class; they were either poor students, or former N.C.O.s of the imperial armies, or just humble men who had had enough of the Bourbons and the *émigrés*. There were practically no working men in it.

The *Charbonnerie* had no principles and no programme. It expressed not the hopes but the regrets and the resentments of its members. It was opposed to the restored dynasty, it hated the *émigrés* and it was suspicious of the church. It was the product of feelings that have been strong in France ever since the first revolution: jealousy of privilege and excessive wealth, contempt for the great by inheritance who could not raise France to the high position that was hers under Napoleon (when the humblest men made the most splendid careers), and anti-clericalism. These feelings, more perhaps than any specific hopes and doctrines, inspired the French republicans from 1815 to 1871.

The *Charbonnerie* was a revolutionary association. It was organised as a system of groups that could multiply quickly and easily. Each group had only twenty members, and was called a *vente*, from the Italian word *venti*, which means twenty. At the head of the organisation was the *suprême vente*, below it the *ventes centrales*, and below them, at the lowest level, the *ventes particulières*. None of these groups was in touch with any other group on its own level but only with the group immediately above it. The members of different groups were quite unknown to each other. It was hoped in this way to combine the greatest efficiency with secrecy and centralised control.

At the time that the *Charbonnerie* was swiftly expanding, in 1821, the liberals were getting the worst of their parliamentary struggle with the ultras. The narrow electorate probably preferred them to their more extravagant and incalculable rivals, but the ultras had used the White Terror immediately following Waterloo to entrench themselves in the prefectures and provincial administrations generally. They found it easy to put pressure on a timid electorate. The liberals were afraid of losing hold altogether of the political machine. They knew the king disliked the ultras, not because he was a convert to limited monarchy but because he was afraid their extravagance would provoke another revolution. The king was growing old and would soon be succeeded by his brother, the acknowledged leader of the ultras. The liberals were therefore in a hurry to prove to Louis XVIII that his fear was well-founded. They themselves believed that, if the ultras became undisputed masters of France, there would be a revolution. Their wisest policy was to seek alliance with the revolutionaries, and in the *Charbonnerie* they saw the organisation destined to overthrow the dynasty. They therefore joined it and even persuaded Lafayette to accept its presidency.

The *Charbonnerie*, together with another and purely Bonapartist revolutionary organisation, the *Chevaliers de la Liberté*, prepared for a great revolt that was to break out all over France in December 1821. Their plan was too ambitious and the premature arrest of some of the conspirators wrecked it. There were risings in two or three places but they were easily suppressed. When the government came to punish the conspirators, it took care not to touch any of the important persons, like Lafayette and the liberal leaders. The impunity of the great naturally turned the others against them, and indeed was intended to discourage them from taking part in plots in which only the humble stood to suffer.

The failure of the great plot ruined the *Charbonnerie*. It put an end, until just before the July revolution, to all relations between the liberals and the republicans. It had also two other important effects. It diverted the minds of the students, always the most active and enterprising members of the *Charbonnerie*, from conspiracy to social theory; and it caused them to seek the alliance of the workers instead of the liberals.

Bazard, the founder of the *Charbonnerie*, became a disciple of Saint-Simon. He became a disciple after Saint-Simon's death, but he was soon the most effective and persuasive of them all. While Saint-Simon was alive, he had converted only a few persons to his doctrines, and some of them, estranged by his mysticism, had deserted him before he died. Soon after his death in 1825, the disciples who had remained loyal were joined by Bazard and Enfantin, whose powers of attraction and administrative ability were greater than Saint-Simon had possessed. Under their new leaders, the disciples of Saint-Simon formed a group of mystics and intellectuals who, though they never contrived to be popular, were to become the most influential of all French schools of socialism. They founded one journal after another, all of them short-lived; but, more important than any of their ventures in the press, were a series of lectures they gave in Paris, later published under the title *The Exposition of the Doctrine of Saint-Simon*. The important lecturer and real expositor was Bazard, who very greatly simplified the master's teaching, distorting it in the process, but also making it more easily understood. Bazard's services to Saint-Simon were greater than those of Engels to Marx. Marx, after all, was a great journalist and pamphleteer. But Saint-Simon, for all his originality and acuteness, was always long-winded, tedious and obscure.

Later on, when Bazard left and Enfantin became the only father of the school or sect of Saint-Simon, the group ceased altogether to be rationalist. It sank, not altogether gently, into the ridiculous, to the great embarrassment of the many serious men who had taken it seriously. But while Bazard was with it, though it appealed to the emotions, it never neglected the critical intelligence. The school of Saint-Simon was not popular; it won no adherents among the workers nor even the lower middle class. Its appeal was always to the intellectuals; whether serious or silly, it was always what we should nowadays call highbrow.

The sect of Saint-Simon, never large and soon ridiculous, was nevertheless of the greatest importance. Most of the persons attracted to it later repudiated it, and they usually did so only a year or two, or even a few months, after their conversion. There was never a doctrine of Saint-Simon for which men were willing to live and to die. And yet his teaching and that of his disciples was certainly the greatest doctrinal influence in the history of French socialism, until it too began to be affected by Marxism. Saint-Simon and Bazard were men of ideas. Though they could not keep the loyalty of their disciples or win the respect of their audiences, they could awaken their social consciences and engage their minds on problems that had seldom or never interested European governments. Even Marx learnt more from Saint-Simon than from any other socialist writer.

Neither the followers of Saint-Simon nor Fourier and his disciples, who preached a social doctrine that was even more remote and fantastic, were politically important before the July monarchy. Their ideas were in the air, but it was still an air breathed only by a select minority of Frenchmen. Before they could move men to political action, these ideas would need to be transformed, to be brought into closer relations with the hopes and fears of the workers, to be reduced to slogans to which men unfamiliar with ideas could easily respond. This process of transmutation occurred under the July monarchy. Saint-Simon and Fourier, the greatest of French socialists if we have in mind the originality, fecundity and subtlety of their theories, were men whose names were always of little account to the workers of France. The slogans they needed they could get more easily from Cabet, Louis Blanc and Proudhon, men still unheard of in 1830.

The students who, after the failure of the *Charbonnerie*, turned their attention to the workers of Paris, were not disciples of Saint-Simon. The doctrines of Saint-Simon attracted only those students who had given up active politics. The others were republicans and democrats who thought they could find in the workers loyal allies as willing to take risks as they were themselves. That is not to say that these students, when they got to know the workers, continued to be as uninterested in social questions as they had been before. On the contrary, their sympathies were immediately awakened; and if, for want of a theory readily at their disposal, they did not become socialists, they became ardent social reformers. They could not say what exactly should be done to help the workers, but they were certain that the first duty of any really popular government must be to improve their lot. And they did what they could to persuade the workers that except in a democracy, which to them meant a republic, they could find no relief. Thus it was that before socialism, or anything that looked like socialism, had permeated down to the people, there was created in Paris an alliance between students and workers, a militant alliance in the name of democracy and the republic.

The middle twenties were a period of discouragement for the republicans. The *Charbonnerie* had failed. The theories of Saint-Simon and propaganda among the workers were mere substitutes for the more hopeful and exciting activities of former days. But even during the years of discouragement, the republicans never ceased to prepare for revolution. They formed secret societies. In November 1827 they took part in an insurrection in Paris when, for the first time since the seventeenth century (since the days of the Fronde), barricades were built in the streets. It was on this occasion that Blanqui, the most famous active revolutionary of the nineteenth century, then a young man of twenty-two, first took up arms against the established government. Blanqui was destined to become a professional revolutionary, perhaps the first of his kind. He spent almost the whole of his long life (he died in 1881) either in prison or in plotting insurrection. In 1827 he was still a student, and he was not to become a socialist till seven or eight years later. He had, however, under the influence of Buonarotti, one of the survivors of Babeuf's conspiracy, already become a revolutionary. Blanqui was the perfect example of a species of revolutionary not uncommon in France. He fought in 1827 without quite knowing what he was fighting for. It was years afterwards that he acquired an ideology, and even then he saw to it that it was as brief and negative as possible. I shall have more to say about it later.

Blanqui was three times wounded on the barricades in November 1827; but he had beginner's luck, and was not taken prisoner. He escaped, and soon afterwards became a teacher at a girls' boarding school, where he fell in love with one of his pupils, whom he later married.

These early secret societies and student-worker insurrections were not very formidable affairs. Before the students and workers could be strong enough to overthrow the weakest and most unpopular of French kings, they had to renew their old alliance with the liberals. But by that time the liberals were themselves stronger and more determined than they had been ten years earlier. A generation of younger liberals were now active, more democratic and more enterprising than their elders, who believed not only that the ultras must be resisted but also that resistance could not be effective until politics were less selfish and less corrupt. They also believed that nothing could reduce this selfishness and corruption except a considerable extension of the franchise. These young liberals and moralists founded two newspapers, the *Globe* and the *National*, both of some importance in the political history of France. At about the same time there were published the first histories and memoirs of the revolutionary and Napoleonic epoch. These books had a great influence on just the class of people on whose loyalty the restored Bourbons would have to depend if their dynasty were to survive—on the students, journalists, lawyers, intellectuals and younger members of the educated classes, not only in Paris but all over France. These early historians of what was, after all, the most interesting and glorious period of French history could not hide their admiration for the great figures of the immediate past. Their younger readers, who scarcely remembered Napoleon and had seldom heard talk of the first republic, were mightily impressed. They were not, perhaps, a large class of people, but they would soon form a considerable part of the narrow electorate. France, they argued, was now a parliamentary monarchy on the English model, and she was a much duller, more corrupt and less formidable country on that account. France had her own history, her own conceptions of justice, equality and good government. As democrats and patriots, these young men were unwilling to take lessons from England. It was bad enough to have been defeated by an alliance of which the English were the backbone; it was unpardonable to look to them for an example. Patriotism in nineteenth-century France has never been the stronger for love of the Bourbons and parliamentary monarchy. It has been at heart either Bonapartist or republican. The French nobility and clergy have often been devoted to their mother country, even when she treated them badly; but in spite of that devotion, because so many exiled nobles and even priests were the enemies of France during the most glorious period of her history, because they were loyal to the Bourbons when such loyalty was disloyalty to France, modern French patriotism has always had about it something of hostility to the old dynasty and the church. A burst of patriotic feeling was therefore always dangerous to the Bourbons. To some Frenchmen, indeed, the July revolution was not only the destruction of a monarchy that threatened to become absolute; it was also an act of revenge for Waterloo.

The revolution could not happen until the alliance between the republicans and liberals, destroyed by the failure of the *Charbonnerie*, was renewed. Neither of the allies was enamoured of the other. Distrust, resentment, and contempt, these were the emotions that kept them apart in spite of their common hostility to the ultra-royalists. It was fear of reaction that had created the first liberal-republican alliance, of which the *Charbonnerie* had been the first consequence and the first casualty. A much stronger fear of reaction than had sufficed in 1820 would be needed to renew the alliance between the two groups who now had more reasons than ever for disliking each other. Not until 1830 could they sink their differences and act together.

In the early 1820s, the ultra-royalists were led by the only real statesman among them, the comte de Villèle. Villèle had been a fanatical ultra in 1815. His first loyalty was always to the class he belonged to by birth. But from 1815 until 1821, when he became Prime Minister, he had had time to think. His loyalties and antipathies were still the same; it was less his feelings than his understanding of France that had changed. He was determined to do what he could for his class and for the church allied to it; he differed from the other ultra-royalists only in thinking that much less was now possible than they had all hoped when they first came back to France. Villèle was a moderating influence. If the ultras behaved intelligently during the last years of Louis XVIII's reign, it was because he acted on their behalf.

But in September 1824 Louis XVIII died. His successor was Charles X, the real leader of the ultras and the first French Bourbon of whom it could truly be said, that he had learnt nothing and forgotten nothing. The new king, like his brother before him, was an old man when he came to the throne. Age had improved his morals but not his understanding. Villèle, who was a legitimist and a nobleman before he was anything else, adopted, though his own opinions were now more moderate, a reactionary policy better pleasing to his new master. As soon as Charles X was king, the *émigrés*, who had reluctantly given up the idea of getting back their land, began to clamour for compensation for its loss. It was decided that they should receive an indemnity of a thousand million francs. Whether this sum were raised by issuing a loan or in any other way, it was certain that the main burden of the transaction would fall on the middle class. The middle class, especially the upper middle class, most strongly represented in the liberal party, had made more out of the revolution than anyone else. It was not unreasonable for the ultras to decide that, if their claims were just, they should be met by the people best able to meet them. But the liberals were determined to do what they could to resist this attack on their property.

The new king's accession also encouraged the pretensions of the clergy. The church was still very popular. Indeed, there were probably far more good Catholics in France than there were royalists, Bonapartists or republicans. But this did not mean that the church was not also very unpopular. There was nothing, except measures directly affecting their property or material well-being, that excited Frenchmen more than legislation either in favour of or against the church. The attitude of Frenchmen to the church was so various, that anything done to her must have consequences not easily predictable. The peasants were devoted to their priests and to the simple beliefs and ceremonies inherited from the past. Anti-clericalism among them was not common until much later in the century. On the other hand, the peasants were indifferent to a great deal that educated Catholics took seriously. Their only contact was with their parish priests. What happened to the religious orders; whether they were allowed to exist, to inherit property, or to open schools; whether the Pope's authority in the church grew weaker or stronger; all these questions, that seemed important to educated and devout Catholics, to them meant nothing. The harsh measures against refractory priests had, during the first revolution, been one of the chief causes of peasants' revolts against the government of the republic. But the French state during the nineteenth century left the secular priests alone; it did nothing, therefore, that could outrage the religious feelings of the peasants. On the other hand, nothing that it did *for* the religious orders could offend the peasants until much later, when the republicans began to win widespread support in the villages.

The upper middle class, later on in the century, when they needed every possible ally against radical republicanism and socialism, were reconciled to the church. But from 1815 to 1830 they were still loyal to the anti-clericalism that the first revolution inherited from the eighteenth century. They were still disciples of Voltaire. They were anxious that the universities and secondary schools, to which only the well-to-do could afford to send their children, should not be dominated by the church. They were therefore hostile to the religious orders and to the higher clergy, whose influence on the government and whose political ambitions were much greater than those of the parish priests. This hostility was the stronger because the ultra-royalists were the allies of the church. Before the revolution, the nobles, though their younger sons and brothers received the most lucrative benefices, had been as much amused by Voltaire as the middle class. They too had believed that religion was excellent for the poor who could not afford a good education. But since then they had suffered with the church and had also noticed that the people were far more devoted to the church than to themselves. The decay of religion had, they now believed, ruined the old society where they held the first places. They must now do what they could to restore the influence and prestige of the church; and when their leader became king of France, they thought their opportunity had come.

Charles X and the ultra-royalists had hoped to get their way without resorting to unconstitutional methods. Villèle had already for some years successfully coaxed and intimidated the narrow circles, much more bourgeois than aristocratic, which alone were politically active in France. Why should not Charles X, with Villèle to back him, be equally successful? Sugar the pill of reaction only a little and the timid liberals, mildly protesting, would in the end swallow it. What Charles X forgot was that Villèle, with the pacific and somnolent Louis XVIII to advise him, had moved slowly and cautiously. It was not an easy thing, with the instruments at that time at the disposal of the French state, to coerce and intimidate even an electorate of 100,000, all of them substantial men and taxpayers, and at whose expense the *émigrés* hoped to be compensated. The liberals were also encouraged by the reactions of the lower middle class and the workers to the king's policy. The lower middle class were mostly either Bonapartists or republicans; that is to say, they either believed that the church must be kept within the limits set for her by Napoleon or else they were anti-clericals. The workers, especially in Paris, were already republicans; they resented the new concessions made or about to be made to the church.

The electorate was so much more bourgeois than aristocratic that only fear could enable the ultra-royalists to dominate it. Villèle had taken care that this fear should exist; and he had also taken care that no greater fear should destroy it. But now this greater fear was brought to birth. The well-to-do businessmen, who were the majority of the electors, were at last more frightened by the consequences of reactionary laws than by the displeasure of the prefects and chiefs of police. The revival of liberalism, the inevitable effect of this fear, irritated the government into taking even more drastic measures. The Paris National Guard, the organisation dearest to the bourgeoisie because it was their security against both reaction and social revolution, was abolished in April 1827; and the censorship was re-established only two months later. The government then dissolved the chamber, in the hope that the electors, properly intimidated, would vote as the king pleased. But the electors, in spite of all the pressure and the tricks used against them, returned a liberal majority. The elections of 1827 persuaded Charles X that he could never get his way by constitutional means; they also persuaded the liberal leaders that, without the moral support of classes not yet enfranchised, the upper middle class, in spite of their numerical superiority, could not get the better of the king and the ultra-royalists.

For the time being Charles X accepted the verdict of the small section of his people interested in his activities. He dismissed Villèle and for nineteen months tolerated a moderate royalist ministry supported by the liberals. But in August 1829 he dismissed this ministry, and replaced it by another so reactionary that everyone expected the early destruction of constitutional government. In the words of de Broglie, the nation saw the *coup d'état* written on the forehead of the government. The Chambers, as soon as they met in March 1830, voted an address to the king, by 221 votes to 181, asking him to dismiss his ministers. A few days later the king prorogued Parliament, and on May 16th he dissolved the lower chamber and ordered new elections.

The struggle between the ultra-royalists and the opposition turned on the re-election of the 221 deputies who had voted for the address offensive to the king. The liberals were determined to secure their re-election, the ultras to prevent it. The royalist newspapers argued that if the electors returned the 221 offenders, their action would imply a renunciation of their right to vote. They had no right to choose deputies to whom the king objected. Charles X himself issued a proclamation to the electors inviting them to choose persons on whose co-operation he could count. *L'Universel*, the newspaper representing the views of the Prime Minister, Polignac, declared that, after the king's proclamation, any of the 221 seeking re-election would automatically become rebels. The king and Polignac expected a sweeping victory for the Right; but it was the liberal opposition that triumphed, returning almost twice as many deputies as the government.

Defeat at the polls did not make the king despair. The electors mostly belonged to one class, a small, selfish and unpopular minority of the nation. A French army had just captured Algiers. Charles X still believed that if he attempted a *coup d'état*, the nation would accept it. Charles X had seen Louis XVI lose his throne. Louis had lost it, thought Charles, because he had hesitated, because he had not taken decisive action in good time. On these occasions boldness was all. So Charles and Polignac acted. On July 26th they published ordinances dissolving the Chamber, altering the electoral law, ordering new elections, and muzzling the press.

But the *coup d'état* had been too long expected. The liberals acted promptly and they were loyally supported by their repub-lican allies. The *National*, the organ of the younger liberals, brought out a special edition, calling upon tax-payers to refuse to pay taxes; and it also published a manifesto, prepared by Thiers and others, declaring that a legal government no longer existed

D

and that force alone ruled in France. The liberals did not expect the dynasty to fall; they merely hoped that open talk of violence would frighten the king and cause him to dismiss Polignac.

The liberals had underestimated their allies. A student organisation, formed as late as January 1830 and of which Lafayette and Auguste Fabre, the editor of the *Tribune*, had been chosen leaders, had decided to fight. Fabre, the real leader of the organisation, gave the order, on the evening of July 27th, to build barricades in the streets of Paris. Where the students led, the workers quickly followed; and there were soon in existence twelve committees in the twelve districts of Paris to co-ordinate resistance and to organise the sending of food, arms and ammunition to the fighters. The government had not expected armed revolt and took no measures to suppress it until it was too late. By the evening of July 28th all the eastern parts of Paris were in the hands of the insurgents. The next day the government fled from Paris, and it was not till then that the liberal deputies allied themselves openly with the insurgents. Meeting at the house of the banker Lafitte (who had helped bring back the Bourbons) they put Lafayette at the head of the revived National Guard, nominated a general to take over command of the troops that had gone over to the insurgents and appointed a municipal commission of five (all of them wealthy and respectable men) to take over the government of Paris. Lafayette addressed a proclamation to the people, in which he mentioned neither Charles X nor a republic. The king had lost Paris almost before he knew he was attacked; and as no one outside Paris seemed willing to fight for him, he left the country as quickly as he could.

Chapter Three

THE JULY MONARCHY

I. REPUBLICANS AND LIBERALS

THERE were few people who regretted Charles X and his *émigré* friends. They had returned to France in 1814, and since then they had seemed intruders from the past in a century that was not theirs, ghosts who behaved like men, who caused anxiety and yet could not be taken quite seriously. With their departure, France was left once again what the revolution had made her.

But though Charles was not regretted, those who drove him from his throne were not loved. There never was a revolution that meant less to most Frenchmen than the one of which he was the victim. A small minority had triumphed over a smaller one. There was nothing here to interest the great majority of Frenchmen, whose property had not been in danger nor their political rights in question. The July revolution was a play in which only the actors and a very small part of the audience were interested. Most of the audience had, indeed, paid so little attention to it that they had not noticed who played the decisive part. The king had fled, his party were powerless and silent, the liberals had triumphed; these were facts that could not escape the most indifferent. But hardly anyone noticed what the republicans, what the students and workers of Paris had done.

The republicans had few illusions about the nature of their victory. They had done the fighting knowing that others must gain more from their victory than they could hope to do themselves. The students who had fought with the workers on the barricades had known that France was afraid of a republic and that they were too weak to impose one on her. They had persuaded the workers to go to battle to the slogan "Long live the

35

Charter." The important thing had been not to frighten the middle class, of whom some had supplied money and arms to the insurgents. It was not till the success of the revolution was assured that the republicans began to regret their early tactics and to clamour for a republic. They thought they had under-estimated their own power; and now that victory was won, they resented that others should gain more by it than they did.

But by that time it was too late. The liberals were much quicker to exploit victory than to fight. Already on July 30th, when at last in the streets of Paris the cry "Long live the republic" was heard more frequently than "Long live the Charter," Thiers had put up placards, declaring that the provinces would not tolerate a republic and mentioning the Duke of Orleans as often as he could. He had chosen his moment skilfully. The liberals had hoped to frighten the king, not to get rid of him. But now that he had fled, how could they resist the cry for a republic, especially as Lafayette, the best-known man in France, was known to be in theory a republican? Thiers helped them in their greatest need. The provinces, he said, would not tolerate a republic. To insist on a republic was therefore to create a danger of civil war. Besides, the men on the barricades had cried out "Long live the Charter"; they had taken up arms to defend the constitution against a reactionary king and not to impose a new régime on the country. If Charles had fled, so much the better. France could find another king, a member of the royal house and yet the son of a regicide, the Duke of Orleans, who could be trusted to respect the constitution. Charles X's flight had given the republicans what seemed like an unexpected opportunity. They had tried to take it, but Thiers had forestalled them. Knowing their real weakness, they allowed themselves to be pushed gently where they did not want to go. When Thiers persuaded Lafayette to appear on a balcony with the Duke of Orleans, the constitutional issue was virtually settled. France was to remain a monarchy, a parliamentary monarchy on the approved English model.

The republicans had given in on the main issue, they had accepted the Duke of Orleans. As a reward for their compliance, they expected other concessions. They wanted a constituent assembly to give France a more democratic constitution, and they asked also for the abolition of the hereditary peerage. They had fought too recently on the barricades to be refused point-blank. It was still thought wise to be polite to them. But their demands were not taken seriously. They had fought for the Charter and therefore in defence of the existing system. They had no business to ask for more now than they had been content to put up with only a few days before. So said the older liberals, who were at pains to prove there had been no revolution. According to them, Charles had abdicated because he had failed to make a revolution, because the defenders of the Charter had been too quick for him. Otherwise, everything remained as it had been before, except that the illegalities and tricks that had kept the liberals out of their inheritance were now done away with.

Not only the republicans, but also the younger liberals who took their opinions from the *Globe* and the *National*, were disgusted by what they called the selfishness of the older liberals. They had also thought the electorate too narrow to give France stable and clean government. They too wanted a new constitution. Besides, they had seen the republicans do the fighting and the old men exploit their victory. They had noticed how the older liberals had kept away from the insurgents until victory was assured, and how soon, after getting what they wanted, they again abandoned them. Towards the end of Charles X's reign, the milder republicans had formed an association, *Aide-toi, le Ciel t'aidera*, which the liberals had joined in great numbers until it had become more liberal than republican. But soon after the July revolution, the liberals deserted this association. Their desertion was the sign that, in their opinion, a temporary and tactical alliance had fulfilled its purpose and must now come to an end. They had taken a risk when risks were worth taking, but now it was once again wiser to be prudent. This policy shocked the younger liberals, who had not yet learned to calculate the uses to which wise men can put their more embarrassing friends. They deserted liberalism and became republicans. Throughout the July Monarchy, the *National*, except when it was suppressed, was the chief organ of the moderate republicans, of men who professed to dislike anarchy, to love democracy and to feel sympathy with the workers. These moderate republicans were men very different from the republicans of before 1830. They were not poor students and workers; they belonged by birth to the well-to-do and educated middle-class. By turning republican after the revolution of 1830, they expressed their preference for the men who had fought on the barricades over those who had exploited their victory. But it was to the latter, to the older liberals, that they were closer by education and social origin. They were mostly young men tired of their elders, in love with their country, generous by temperament, and anxious that France should have just and clean government. As they came to know more of the great revolution, they found it easy to identify themselves with the Girondins, who were also of good family, patriotic, believers in political democracy, private property and the rights of man, and haters of anarchy and mob rule. Later on, as the July Monarchy grew older, the rank and file supporters of the moderate republicans belonged mostly to the lower middle class, the class that would get the vote if ever the moderates got their way. But the leaders still came from the upper middle class, though they were professional men rather than bankers, merchants or industrialists. They were still in 1848 what they became in 1830, respectable idealists, admirers of the Gironde, more interested in words than in things, or, if you prefer it, in ideas than in facts.

II. THE FOUR KINDS OF REPUBLICANS

The history of the revolutionary movement, republican and socialist, during the July Monarchy is much more complicated and important than during the Restoration. It is not possible to give a short and completely adequate account of it. If I am to explain as much as I can of it without creating too much confusion, I must classify and sub-divide. I must choose between two evils; and I hope I have done rightly in choosing to risk misleading rather than confusing the reader. I want to classify the republicans and socialists into four main groups, and divide the July Monarchy into three periods. But before I do this, I must insist that there never were four groups actually existing and easily distinguishable from one another. There were during the July Monarchy innumerable societies, most of them very small and short-lived, and there were even more newspapers with tiny circulations and often only a few months or weeks of life. To follow at all ade-

quately the activities of these societies and newspapers, except in
a book of many volumes, is quite impossible; and yet it was these
societies and newspapers that interested contemporaries. The
four classes into which I have divided them meant nothing to most
of the people who belonged to the societies and read the papers.
They represent only tendencies that historians looking back at the
July Monarchy have thought they could discern. More than one
classification is possible, but the one I have adopted is, I think, the
most useful; it takes notice of the divisions that are apt to be
most important in times of revolution.

The four groups I have in mind are: (1) the moderate republicans, (2) the Jacobins or radicals, (3) the social reformers, and
(4) the revolutionaries.

(1) Of the moderate republicans I have already spoken, when
I was explaining how the younger liberals, after the July revolution, abandoned their elders (whom they had never admired) and
became republicans. I need say no more now than that the
moderates very soon became the largest group of republicans in
the country. They were the least dangerous and most respectable,
and to this they owed their numerical superiority. They were the
only republicans willing to co-operate with the regular parliamentary opposition. Their principal newspaper was *Le
National*, and they dominated two important societies, *Aide-toi, le
Ciel t'aidera* and the *Association for the Liberty of the Press*. As long
as open opposition to the régime was possible, they were active;
and what they did was taken more notice of than the activities
of other republicans. In times of repression or of republican
apathy, they alone were still represented in the Chamber and the
more public press. They were the most presentable and therefore
the most visible republicans; they were never altogether submerged, even at the height of reaction.

(2) The Jacobins[1] or radicals, like the moderates, believed in
republicanism, in manhood suffrage and in social reform. Like the
moderates, they were not quite sure what social reforms they
wanted. They too were more interested in political than in social
questions. It might seem that they were too much like the moder-

[1] I use this word only because it suggests the bias of this class of republicans.
The groups or individuals belonging to it did not usually call themselves Jacobins
though other people often gave them that name.

ates to be worth distinguishing from them. The difference between them was certainly less a difference of doctrine than of temperament. But it was an important difference, to which their very different behaviour after the revolution of 1848 bears witness. The Jacobin leaders were also of bourgeois origin, but in 1848 they proved that their sympathy with the workers was as strong as their loyalty to their class. They were not admirers of the Gironde, but of Robespierre and Marat, the Convention and the Commune. Their strength was in Paris. They were not professional revolutionaries. They preferred reform and peaceful propaganda to plots and violence. But when plots and violence prevailed, they were more inclined to blame the authorities than the plotters. They had an uneasy feeling that to abandon the workers and the men at the barricades was treachery, a betrayal of the republic and of the great revolution. They did not like the Terror of 1793–4 but they were willing to excuse the terrorists; they hoped that, unlike their hero Robespierre, they need not resort to violence to achieve their ends; but if it should come to violence, they hoped they knew their duty. The radicals also had a following in the lower middle class, especially among the poorer and more embittered sections of that class; and through these sections they were in close touch with the workers. They did not, like the moderates, sympathise with the workers from far off and praise them while they behaved according to the standards of the younger and more tolerant bourgeois; they understood the workers, and were even anxious that the workers should understand and like them. The moderates, on the other hand, retained much more of the upper class mentality: they thought their opinion of the workers mattered more than the workers' opinion of them. Should the workers disappoint them they would be annoyed; but the Jacobins were at least as anxious that they should not disappoint the workers.

The Jacobins, unlike the moderates, had very little to do with the parliamentary opposition. They were much more closely in touch with groups yet more radical than themselves. They controlled two important associations: the *Friends of the People* and the *Society for the Rights of Man*, to which many professed revolutionaries also belonged. The most prominent of the radical leaders during the early years of the July Monarchy was Godefroy

Cavaignac, who died in 1845. He was succeeded by Ledru-Rollin, perhaps the most important of French republicans before the republic was finally established in 1870. The most influential newspapers controlled by the radicals were, immediately after the July revolution, the *Tribune* (whose editor Fabre had set the workers and students in motion on July 27th); and then, from 1843 onwards, the *Réforme*. I give these facts rather drily at present, but it will be seen later that they are important.

(3) By social reformers I mean the men who, whether they were socialists or not, put social questions before political ones. Democracy, they said, is at best only a means to an end more important than itself, which is to secure for the poor a degree of material welfare that will enable them to live decently. Some people, like the disciples of Saint-Simon who got control of the *Globe* newspaper after the July revolution, had no use for democracy. Like the disciples of Fourier, they expected that society would be reorganised from above. In the history of socialist thought, the schools of Saint-Simon and Fourier occupy an important place. But their direct influence on politics was small. They did almost nothing to ensure that there was an effective popular demand for either socialism or social reform. As I am dealing only with popular movements, I have nothing to say about either of these schools, except that their influence, indirect though it was and passing through minds less subtle than their own, was much greater during the July Monarchy than it had been before 1830.

The first social reformer who was more than a name to the Paris workers was Raspail. He was neither a doctrinaire nor a politician. By profession he was a scientist and a practising doctor, a fore-runner of Pasteur and one of the founders of micro-chemistry. His work brought him into contact with the poor, and he soon decided that nothing could be done to help them until they were taught to help themselves, to organise politically and to secure allies, until they became so strong that it was no longer safe to ignore their demands. Raspail was not a demagogue or a revolutionary; he cared nothing for the heroes of the first republic and was not personally ambitious. He was an indignant scientist who found it hard to forgive the rich for their indifference to the poor. Though he was not in the ordinary sense a politician, he was certainly politically active. He was a prominent member of the *Friends of the People*, an association dominated by the radical republicans. He ran for a time his own newspaper, the *Réformateur*, in which he advocated manhood suffrage, pacifism, agricultural co-operation, progressive taxation and prison reform. He thought all these things measures of social hygiene; society was sick and must be restored to health. It was sometimes necessary to be a little rough, if men, especially men in high position, were to be brought to their senses. Raspail did not always use kid gloves (he took part in two revolutions—1830 and 1848), but he was not a professed revolutionary and he did not believe in the class war. Among the workers of Paris he held for years a unique position: he was the object of their affection, trust and gratitude.

Socialism properly so called, by which I mean any theory advocating social control of the economy to prevent the exploitation of the poor by the rich, had hardly affected the workers before the 1840s. Saint-Simon died in 1825, Bazard in 1832, Fourier in 1837; the three fathers of French socialism were dead before most of the workers had heard of doctrines whose chief purpose was their welfare. It was not until the latter part of Louis Philippe's reign that socialist propaganda began to take effect. Fourier's disciple, Victor Considérant, was active from 1832 onwards; and Pierre Leroux, who learned his socialism from Saint-Simon and Bazard, even earlier. They were both writers more easily understood by the general public than the more gifted men whose ideas they made popular.

Yet it was not Considérant and Leroux who converted the Paris workers to socialism. This conversion, which was to have such important consequences during the second republic, was the work of Cabet and Louis Blanc. Cabet was a communist in the old-fashioned meaning of the word. He disliked revolution and violence of every kind. "If I held a revolution in my fist," he said, "I would not let it loose, even if it meant my dying in exile." He preached full communism and complete democracy; every man must be paid according to his needs, and everyone exercising authority must be elected. He did not believe that the classes are necessarily hostile to one another. Nor did he condemn Christianity. He thought it a very good religion, as Christ had preached it, but that since his time it had been perverted by the churches. Cabet's most popular book, his *Voyage en Icarie*, was published in 1840. His Sunday newspaper, *Le Populaire*, was widely read by the workers in the thirties, but it was only in the forties, after his return from exile in England, that he used it to preach communism. The police were not frightened of Cabet. He used his influence to keep the workers from violence and he admitted that the communist society he described still lay far in the future. He presented it to the workers as a sort of reward for years of patience and good behaviour. Cabet, thought the police, was a good influence and an antidote to the revolutionaries; he taught the workers to keep quiet and to dream. The police forgot that not all a man's arguments are equally persuasive. The communist society that Cabet described was very different from the Paris known to the workers; it was, so Cabet told them, the only just society. That being so, the society they lived in—which depended so completely on their work and yet rewarded them so badly— that society was unjust and they were its victims. Cabet also advised the workers to be patient. But was this advice equally good? Why must they bear the yoke patiently? They had used violence before and had overturned governments. True, they had gained nothing by violence in the past, because their allies had deceived them. But they had felt their own power; it had been to the interest of the rich to flatter them. Though Cabet preached patience, there were other people with a different message for the workers.

If Cabet taught the workers to dream, Louis Blanc brought them a little closer to reality. He, too, was not a revolutionary, but he did not preach pacifism. He was a friend of the Jacobins and of Ledru-Rollin. Indeed, he was as much a radical republican as a socialist. He did not advocate revolutionary violence, but he greatly admired the Jacobin heroes of 1793–4, the secret of whose power had been their ruthless violence and their popularity with the workers of Paris. The socialism preached by Louis Blanc was milder than Cabet's; the ideal society he described was less unlike contemporary France; and he also believed that it could be established by peaceful methods. Yet the authorities liked him much less than they liked Cabet. Louis Blanc told the workers that, if only the government were willing, a great deal could be done for them in a short time. He did not believe, as Fourier and his disciples had done, that voluntary associations for communal production could succeed. Nor, on the other hand, did he advocate the complete abolition of private property. He took up a position half-way between collectivism and Fourierism. The state, he taught, should control the banks, the large factories, railways and insurance companies, leaving to private enterprise all industries still producing on a small scale. And even in the sphere left to private enterprise, the state must establish co-operatives, or Social Workshops (*Ateliers Sociaux*) as Louis Blanc called them, should the workers want them. The state ought not to control these workshops but ought to provide the capital to establish them.

This theory Louis Blanc developed in a book published in 1839, whose title, *l'Organisation du Travail*, became one of the workers' slogans in 1848. By that time, Louis Blanc was easily the most influential socialist writer in France. Proudhon, who belonged to the same generation as Blanc, was not yet really popular. His influence, that of a socialist who believed in the class war and the destruction of the state, was much greater after than before 1848. For the time being the workers were still willing to listen to a more hopeful and more amiable prophet. In 1830 they had been deceived, and since then a good deal persecuted, but they had not yet been shot down in large numbers in the streets of Paris. The doctrines of the class war and of unrelenting hostility to the bourgeois state did not yet seem as obviously true as they were to seem after June 1848.

(4) The professed revolutionaries, the last group that I have to describe, were as little doctrinaire as any of the republicans. The complicated theories of Proudhon and Marx, at once revolutionary and socialist, were still unknown. Proudhon, no doubt, had already a considerable reputation, he had already asked his famous question about property and had called it theft; but Marx was unheard of. Proudhon dominated French socialism during the third quarter of the nineteenth century, and Marx not until late in the fourth. Before 1848 such revolutionary socialism as existed in France was a matter of conspiracy and adventure much more than doctrine. These revolutionaries were busy forming secret societies and making plots, and they had little time to

discuss social problems. They too had a hero from the days of the first republic, Babeuf, who had prepared a conspiracy against the reactionaries in 1796. A year or two after the July revolution, one of Babeuf's lieutenants, Buonarotti, had described this conspiracy in his book, *La Conspiration des Égaux*. This book soon became the bible of the revolutionaries.

Much the ablest of the revolutionaries was Auguste Blanqui. He was a man who tried to keep innocent of theory as long as he could. In the end, the nineteenth century proved too much for him, and he, too, eventually wrote a book, *La Critique Sociale*, to justify his life. In this book, he explained that it is always harmful to make a plan in advance for proceeding on unknown ground. The revolutionary must let the more remote future take care of itself. A person who makes a feasible plan for the future works out changes to be made in a system that will remain substantially the same. But if his purpose is to destroy that system, it is useless for him to make plans for what will emerge from its ruins. The unknown factors that he cannot take into account are then too many. The object of the revolutionary must therefore be to give mankind another chance, to free men from the trammels of the past so that they can make a new society; it is not for him to anticipate the work of future generations. Now this theory, which Blanqui produced long after he had become a revolutionary, is at bottom only an excuse for doing without a theory altogether. When Blanqui was young, men fought against injustice because they hated it and had energy to spare. As he grew older, he had to compete against the influence of such men as Proudhon and even Marx; and so he produced a theory to justify his past. He was never interested in winning over the multitude. The work of destruction could best be done by a resolute minority; what Blanqui looked for were men as persistent, brave and resourceful as himself, and he knew that they could never be many.

Blanqui was the greatest revolutionary leader of the nineteenth century. He was active from 1827 until 1871. He spent the greater part of his life in prison. While still young, he became a legendary figure. He was relentless; as soon as he was out of prison he was busy forming secret societies and making plots. Men who had often heard of him had seen him only from time to time. When not in prison, he was usually in hiding, except during the short periods, lasting only a few weeks or months and separated from each other by as many years, when the Paris workers were powerful. The sort of dread he inspired when he appeared in a public place can be seen in the passage of de Tocqueville's *Souvenirs*, where he describes the invasion of the national assembly by the Paris mob on May 15th, 1848. To the respectable classes the mere sight of him was a bad omen for France. It was as if they believed that only when the foundations of society were cracking could such a man emerge from the darkness into the light of the sun.

Blanqui was all the more powerful because the rich were frightened of him. He never had more than a few thousand followers, but he was for years the idol of the Paris workers. He was an unseen idol, except during short intervals, and all the more powerful for that. The workers knew other people better and felt greater affection for them, but they felt that Blanqui was formidable, and that the fear he inspired was worth many battalions to them. Repeated failure could not tarnish his reputation or weaken the fear he inspired. As late as the Commune of 1871, when the workers made their greatest bid for independence and power, they still wanted him for their leader, and many of them believed that if he had been in Paris they would not have been so easily defeated.

There were other revolutionaries in France during the July Monarchy, the Creole Barbès, the printer Martin Bernard, and a visionary from Alsace, Aloysius Huber. They were all trusted leaders in their day, but Blanqui was worth more to the "cause" than all of them together.

I have attempted a short account of four classes of republicans and socialists. I cannot pretend that the classification is exhaustive. I have made it for convenience sake and it ought not to be taken too seriously. In any case, it applies much more to the leaders than to their followers. It is the prominent men who, just because they are prominent, are anxious to appear consistent. They have reputations at stake, they have created expectations in the people they have sought to attract to their standards, they have parts to play in the political world. They must, of course, change with the times or else they will lose their influence, but they must not change too quickly. They must be true to their images in other men's minds.

Of these four classes, only one and the smallest was revolutionary by profession. And yet they all belonged, in one way or another, to the revolutionary movement. They were all to play their indispensable parts in the revolution of 1848; they were all enemies of the régime and not merely opponents of the government in power. They all believed—even those among them, the great majority, who disliked the actual noise and sting and smell of violence—in the morality of revolution. What was done by the people or in the people's name had a peculiar sanctity for them. If governments ruled unjustly, if they neglected the great principles of the first revolution and the people were in revolt against them, then what the people did was legitimate and ought to be accepted by all men of good will. To do legal violence to justice is worse than to violate law. Even the moderate republicans, who never preached nor liked violence, subscribed to this principle. They could not shed blood, but there were times when they could be the respectable allies of men who were willing to shed it. They knew men who knew men who could defy and kill the police from a sense of duty. "We must neither do violence nor praise it, but we must not too hastily condemn it; if violence happens, and is popular, and enables us to rule France, we must accept it as an act of judgment on a bad government." Such words as these might express the feelings of the moderate republicans from 1830 until just after the revolution of 1848, when their allies to the left of them began to be troublesome. They are not the words of cowards, but of respectable people with mildly radical sympathies, who would never urge others to take risks they dared not take themselves.

The new Jacobins also refrained from violence, though they praised their spiritual ancestors of the first revolution who had used it. They, too, were not cowards. They took other risks and were persecuted by the police, but they did not believe in street fighting. On the other hand, they were the allies of the students and workers and would not turn against them even when they used violence. As for the social reformers, men like Raspail, Louis Blanc and Proudhon, they had made the workers' cause their own. They never incited to violence, but they either took part in it when they thought it inevitable, or, if they stood aside from the armed struggle, always blamed the government for it. Revolution was a thing to be avoided, but if those who could prevent it by timely reforms refused to do so, it was both necessary and just. These four kinds of republicans saw France divided into two camps, the government and privileged classes on the one hand, and the people, represented by themselves, on the other. The political struggle between the government and the people was not always the same in character; but whenever it degenerated into violence, all the republicans, from the moderates to the revolutionaries, blamed the government.

I have said that these four kinds of republicans were not groups recognised by their contemporaries. They belonged to many different associations; and between these associations there were all kinds of relations. Contemporaries recognised only two broad classes of republicans, the moderates and the radicals or Jacobins. The men I have called social reformers and revolutionaries they thought of as more extreme radicals than the others. The moderates had a considerable following not only in Paris and the other great cities but in many of the smaller towns in every part of France. They were more numerous than all the other republicans put together. The Jacobins, social reformers and revolutionaries, were strongest in Paris, though they also had friends in Lyon and some of the other large industrial towns.

Apart from the republicans, there was a fifth class of men who helped to prepare France for her next revolution. They were the Catholic Liberals. Unlike the four classes of republicans I have tried to describe, they were not the heirs of the great revolution, nor were they in any, even the mildest, sense its apologists. But they were the first Catholics to praise democracy; and their praise could make it respectable in circles that would never have listened to the republicans.

The founder of Catholic Liberalism in France was Lamennais. He first attracted notice as an enemy of Gallicanism. During the Restoration there were still many Gallicans among the higher clergy. They were attacked by two kinds of advocates of liberty for the church: by the Catholics who accepted the political consequences of the revolution and wanted the church free from interference by the state; and by the Catholics who hated the revolution so much that they could not bear to see the church in any way associated with a state tainted by revolution. Bonald, Maistre and Lamennais belonged to this second class. At that time Lamennais cared nothing for democracy, and his only concern was for the freedom and purity of the church.

The revolution of 1830 caused Lamennais to take an interest in the people. The republicans, who claimed to speak for the people, were enthusiasts like himself. He felt a growing sympathy for them. In October 1830, he and his friends, Montalembert and Lacordaire, founded a Catholic and liberal newspaper, *l'Avenir*, in which they preached the complete independence of the church in all matters spiritual, freedom of education, of association and of the press, a decentralised administration, and political democracy. The church, they said, had in her great days been the friend of humanity and freedom. The doctrine she taught was true, and so she had nothing to fear from science and free enquiry; and of her charity she must always be the friend of the people. The church is the gift of God to all men; of all institutions on earth she ought to be the most popular.

The enthusiasm, the violent polemics and the liberalism of *l'Avenir* offended the bishops of France, who used their influence in Rome to prejudice Pope Gregory XVI against Lamennais. He therefore decided to go to the Pope and make a friend of him. He was too simple a man to understand what Rome must think of him. Gregory neither praised nor blamed him but kept him waiting. In the end he grew tired of Roman urbanity and inaction, and decided to return to France. He was in Munich when he heard of the Papal Encyclical, *Mirari Vos*, condemning all his favourite doctrines. At first he submitted, but when the French bishops tried to make his submission more complete than he intended it to be, he revolted. A little later, in 1834, he published his most famous book, *Les Paroles d'un Croyant*, in which he proclaimed himself a full convert to democracy. But democracy in the 1830s meant republicanism.

The Pope issued a special encyclical condemning *Les Paroles d'un Croyant*, and Lamennais left the church. Lacordaire, Montalembert and his other friends could not bring themselves to desert their religion, but they never lost their respect and even a certain tender regard for Lamennais. His influence on his

E

friends was always great, even when they found it impossible to agree with him. Montalembert formed a Catholic parliamentary party, which was at first opposed to the monarchy but soon became reconciled to it. But though it accepted the régime, it consistently opposed all the king's governments. It was more truly liberal than the old liberals had ever been. Montalembert's party, though it was republican for only a short time, was never enamoured of the monarchy. It detached a considerable number of Catholics from loyalty to any particular dynasty, and taught them always to put the interests of the church first, even at the price of an alliance with the republicans.

Lamennais, though he never created a party, did much more for the republican cause than Montalembert. He had a great popularity even among people who never dreamt of following his example. They trusted and admired him, and they learnt to feel some sympathy for what he so warmly praised. He created for republicanism and democracy a kind of sentimental prestige among Frenchmen who were still devout Catholics. He made them familiar with words and arguments that else might have shocked them. He also taught them to dislike the indifference, selfishness, pedantry and hypocrisy of Louis-Philippe's governments. He helped to bring the July Monarchy into contempt with the people. For a few months after February 1848 France took kindly to the republic. The word that was scarcely mentioned in polite circles in 1815, that might have offended the provinces in July 1830, was for a time in everyone's mouth. Though the second republic soon outlived its welcome, that welcome was at first warm and general. France had not exactly wanted the republic, but that she accepted it with so good a grace was largely owing to Lamennais.

III. THE YEARS OF ACTIVITY

I said the revolutionary movement during the July Monarchy could be conveniently divided into three periods. The first period lasted until April 1835. It was during those years that the four great republican associations and a host of republican newspapers were most active. The republicans were able to make what we nowadays call propaganda on a scale never before possible in France to opponents of the established régime. The republicans had been the allies of the new rulers of France against Charles X; together they had proclaimed certain principles, which the liberals could not at once reject merely because they had now ceased to be useful to them. Indeed, the liberals were not much more cynical than other men; they did not at first even wish to abandon their principles. But when they saw how inconvenient these principles had become, how much more the republicans were asking for than had seemed possible to anyone before 1830, they were soon persuaded that the republicans were abusing liberal principles, that they were subverting society and must be stopped. For the republicans were not only asking for a constituent assembly and an extension of the franchise; even the mildest of them would not be content with less than manhood suffrage, while others were clamouring for progressive taxation, the democratisation of the National Guard, free primary schools for the children of the poor and even the granting of credits by the state to needy and deserving persons. The republicans had allowed the July revolution to go to their heads. This reaction of the liberals will seem natural enough if we remember that the republicans were already making demands on behalf of the poor sometimes more drastic than any made by the English Chartists after 1832.

For nine months after the July revolution the authorities let the republicans alone, hoping that it was the excitement of victory which made them pitch their demands so high, and that time would bring them to their senses. But the republicans remained as immoderate as ever, and they were taking advantage of the indulgence granted to them to proselytise the nation. They had founded innumerable newspapers and their great associations were spreading fast. The liberal counter-offensive began early in 1831, when the banker Casimir Périer became Minister of the Interior.

Of the four great republican associations, the two controlled by the moderates, *Aide-toi, le Ciel t'aidera* and the *Association for the Liberty of the Press*, confined themselves to legal activities, though they, too, were sometimes prosecuted by the government. The purpose of these associations was to give financial assistance to republican newspapers, found them where they did not exist, engage counsel to defend them, if they were prosecuted, and pay their fines when necessary. The law restricted the liberty of the press, less than it had done before 1830, but still considerably; and it was also a difficult law to interpret. The government were willing to prosecute frequently in the hope that a fair proportion of the decisions would go in their favour; they were richer than the republicans, and, if this war of wealth against comparative poverty were continued long enough, might hope to ruin the republicans and so reduce them to inactivity. But the republicans, though the strain on their resources sometimes threatened to exhaust them, were not altogether displeased by the government's tactics. Political trials are important public events; the republicans had excellent lawyers in their ranks and they got much more publicity than they needed to pay for, very often at the government's expense.

The other two associations, the two in which the Jacobins predominated, were accounted even more dangerous. They were less powerful in the provinces, but they were strong in Paris and some of the other large towns. Their influence was not confined to the middle class; they attracted many people who had little or no property to lose. Their demands were more extreme, and they were more likely to be captured by the revolutionaries.

The *Friends of the People* (*Amis du Peuple*) was never a large association. It never had more than about 600 members, including not only radical republicans but Raspail and Blanqui. For a time, during the Casimir Périer Ministry, it worked for the violent overthrow of the government. But during the last and most dangerous period of its existence, when it was presided over by Raspail, it gave up all thought of violence. Under Raspail's direction, each member of the association was made responsible for the welfare of six poor families, undertaking to educate the children, to find work for the parents and medical assistance for them all. It also printed pamphlets and news-sheets, dealing with the most severely practical problems. Its propaganda was all the more effective because it paid so little attention to general principles and was content to describe the sufferings of the poor and the indifference of the authorities. It presented facts that no one could deny and left it to its readers to draw their own conclusions. The *Friends of the People* was an association confined to

Paris; its members all belonged to the middle class, but it was in the closest touch with 3,600 working-class families. And its prestige among the workers extended much further than the actual help it could give them. The authorities reserved their hardest blows for this association. Four major political trials involved leaders of the *Amis du Peuple*. The evidence against them was so flimsy that juries would not convict. But the association was felt to be too dangerous to be tolerated. At the last trial, though its leaders were acquitted, the association was dissolved by order of the President of the Court. He could afford to take this action because a recent insurrection, though it was impossible to implicate the *Friends of the People*, had frightened the middle class and had set public opinion against the republicans.

The *Society of the Rights of Man*, though it was formed in 1831, only became important in 1833 after the suppression of the *Friends of the People*. It was not confined to Paris, and was therefore a rival of the two great moderate republican associations. If you count only the size of its audiences, it was not a very formidable rival. You will find nothing on the scale of English Chartism in the France of Louis-Philippe. But the *Society of the Rights of Man*, though small, was dangerous. The new French ruling-class and their sympathisers were not more numerous than the ruling-class in England. They, too, were only a small minority of the people, and they lacked many of the advantages enjoyed by the rulers of England. They were new to the business of government, they were not accustomed to be obeyed, they could not count on the traditional loyalty of the people, and they had to control restless minorities that had several times resorted to violence in the last fifty years. And so, French governments were perhaps even more frightened of the republicans than English governments of the much more numerous Chartists.

To suppress the *Friends of the People* the authorities had made use of Article 291 of the Penal Code, forbidding unauthorised associations of more than twenty persons. The *Society of the Rights of Man* therefore decided to reorganise themselves into sections of from ten to twenty members. This type of organisation, giving perforce a considerable independence to the sections, made more evident the differences of opinion within the society. Most of the sections and the Central Committee were controlled by the Jacobins, while in others the revolutionaries gained the upper hand. The *Friends of the People* had been a bourgeois society offering help and protection to the workers; the *Rights of Man* had many working-class sections. It was the first political association in France, other than a secret society or insurgent organisation, to which bourgeois and workers both belonged. The *Society of the Rights of Man* worked openly and was intended to be permanent and to spread all over France. As a matter of fact, it was never powerful, except in a few of the largest towns. But it did one great service to the republican and radical cause in France; it converted the silk-workers of Lyon, who remained for the rest of the century among the most reliable and combative enemies of every reactionary or conservative government in France.

To destroy the *Society of the Rights of Man*, the government passed early in 1834 a law on Associations, which permitted the authorities to dissolve any political society, even if it was organised in sections of not more than twenty members. This law helped to provoke one of the three great working-class revolts of nineteenth-century France, the Lyon silk-workers' insurrection of April 1834. There had been a silk-workers' strike two months earlier, and just before the strike-leaders were due to stand their trial, news of the law on Associations reached Lyon. The workers, already in an angry mood, looked upon the new law as a provocation. Both the *Society of the Rights of Man* and the government expected trouble, the former advising their Lyon committee to be cautious, and the latter moving ten thousand troops into the town. On April 9th, just as the trial of the strike-leaders was beginning, a shot was fired in the Place St. Jean outside the law courts, and one man among the crowd of workers gathered there was killed. The workers at once withdrew to their own part of the town and began to build barricades. The first barricades were easily taken, and the revolt might perhaps have been quickly put down if the troops had pressed home their attack. But for some mysterious reason the troops were ordered out of the town, and, when they renewed their attack, four days' fighting, during which many hundreds of men were killed, barely sufficed to defeat the insurgents. There was a sympathetic revolt in Paris, which was much more quickly put down; and also smaller disturbances in other parts of France.

The *Society of the Rights of Man* had not encouraged the workers to revolt; it had foreseen their inevitable defeat. But once the workers had taken to arms, the *Society* supported them. Though it did not direct the revolt, it defended the cause of the workers and abused the authorities. It went out of its way to share the "moral responsibility" (as some people liked to call it) for what the workers had done.

About 2,000 persons were arrested for complicity in these revolts and disturbances, of whom 164 were eventually brought to trial before the House of Peers in May, 1835. This trial, known at the time as the "Procès Monstre," ruined the *Society of the Rights of Man* and also did great damage to the republican cause. It brought into the light of day all the quarrels and jealousies that divided the republicans. The trial, illegal in principle (because the accused ought never to have been brought before the House of Peers) and conducted in a manner more vindictive than decent, also discredited the government. The majority of Frenchmen were by this time heartily sick of their rulers and of the republicans. Had they known how, they would have been glad to get rid of them both. But the fate of majorities is always to be inactive; whatever the outcome of quarrels between minorities, it will hardly ever happen that none survives. For the time being it was the government that got rid of the republicans, or, to come nearer to the truth, drove them underground.

IV. THE YEARS OF SILENCE

The late thirties and early forties must have seemed to contemporaries a dead season for the republican cause. Most of the republican leaders were either in prison or in exile, for though the real offenders, the men actually in touch with the workers, had all been radicals, social reformers or revolutionaries, the moderates had also suffered in the general disgrace. Their most important newspaper, *Le National*, survived, but its brilliant editor, Armand Carrel, had been killed in a duel. The republicans were dull and apathetic; and even when, after the amnesties of 1837 and 1840, their leaders returned, their courage was slow to revive. The returned exiles were, now more than ever, firm believers in moderation and respect for the law; and with such virtues as these, men remain inactive under repressive governments.

There was, however, some activity among the republicans. The bolder spirits among them, that is to say, the radicals and revolutionaries, formed secret societies. About these societies we unfortunately know very little. The moderate republicans resented their existence, believing they did more harm than good to the cause. They were certainly useful to the authorities. By introducing police spies into them it was possible to provoke revolts at the times and places that best suited police headquarters. One of these police spies, Delahodde, later wrote a *History of the Secret Societies*, which, although it is often obviously untruthful, does give us some idea of the conditions they worked in. Delahodde was interested in the revolutionary societies and he was naturally anxious to exaggerate their importance. These secret societies consisted almost entirely, except for a handful of leaders, of working-men. The most violent of them seem to have been the ones most riddled with police spies; and the greatest difficulty that Blanqui, Barbès and the other leaders had to contend with was the incessant clamour for action inspired by men like Delahodde. The workers' insurrection of May 1837 in Paris, a complete failure which led to the arrest and imprisonment until 1848 of both Blanqui and Barbès, was almost certainly due to pressure stimulated by the police. With Blanqui in prison the revolutionary societies became almost completely ineffective, marionettes whose strings were in the hands of the police. But there were other secret societies that were not revolutionary. They were mostly either friendly or educational societies, and some of them undertook to preach communism to the workers. It was to neutralise their influence that Cabet began teaching his own more cautious and more pacific brand of communism. For though many of these societies were not in fact revolutionary, their pamphlets were remarkable for the violence of the language used. They did not, like Cabet, denounce violence; they merely abstained from it for the time being.

V. THE PRELUDE TO REVOLUTION

The last six or seven years of Louis-Philippe's reign—the third of the periods into which I have found it convenient to divide it—were remarkably peaceful. There were no important revolts, except the last one which ended with the overthrow of the régime. There is a resemblance here between the Restoration and the July Monarchy. They were both more troubled by violence in their early than their late years, and the revolts that destroyed them destroyed them easily, though they happened after long periods of social peace.

The most likely explanation is perhaps also the simplest. The repeated violence of the early years gave the authorities allies they might not otherwise have had—the many people who, though they cared nothing for their rulers, wanted law and order firmly established. The great obstacle in the way of revolutionary movements in nineteenth century France has been not the loyalty of the people to their governments but their fear of anarchy. Whenever that fear has been strong, the revolutionaries, despite their activity and successful propaganda among certain classes, have never succeeded in getting their way. It would have been perhaps more to their interest to lessen the number of their enemies than to increase the number of their friends. If this generalisation is true—and I think it is—it explains more than a little the fortunes and misfortunes of the revolutionary cause in France. For the revolutionaries have always over-estimated their strength, attributing their successes much more to themselves than to the weakness of their enemies and the indifference of the people. It is when they have been in a chastened mood, abandoning their more extreme demands and willing to accept respectable alliances, that they have come nearest to success. Unfortunately, as we shall see later, they never understood what conditions made those alliances possible, and therefore always tried to get more out of them than the country was willing to let them have.

Be that as it may, it is clear that in the 1840s the republicans, behaving much more prudently than they had done ten years before, made a remarkable recovery. In 1836 there was only one republican in the Chamber; by 1842 there were six. The republicans in the Chamber were never more than a handful, but their presence in it was important. In the early thirties the larger groups competing for power in the Chamber had all a reasonable chance of getting it. But by the forties the most conservative of these groups, led by Guizot, had established a monopoly of power. Guizot's parliamentary supporters were not even popular with the majority of the narrow electorate; they owed their seats as much to money and influence judiciously expended as to the confidence of the electors. The opponents of Guizot felt themselves permanently excluded from power. If they were to regain it, they must seek allies outside parliament and outside the timid and venal electorate. These allies they could only find through the good offices of the republicans in the Chamber, who had friends willing to take risks to get rid of Guizot. And these friends had other friends, willing to take even greater risks. There was, so to speak, a chain of friendship leading from the respectable republicans in the Chamber to groups they knew nothing of and with whom they would never have consented to deal directly. Along this chain of friendship only the contiguous links were attracted to each other. The chain might be, and indeed had already been, broken in several places; but a successful revolution could not happen until it was whole again. No one, no man or group of men, saw that chain as a whole or worked deliberately to repair it. It was just that when conditions were favourable, the links came naturally together; and they were favourable whenever the people were more tired of their rulers than afraid of anarchy. And this was how France felt for some years before 1830 and before 1848.

During the forties the two most important republican newspapers were *Le National*, the organ of the moderates, and *La Réforme*, the organ of the radicals. It was, of course, the moderates who co-operated with the Gauche Dynastique, the parliamentary opposition to Guizot. In theory, the *National* still wanted a republic and manhood suffrage, but in practice it insisted much more strongly on less extreme demands, demands that were likely to please the Gauche Dynastique and the lower middle class, whose enfranchisement would, so Guizot's opponents believed, destroy his monopoly of power. Guizot's foreign policy, his constant anxiety to please the English, had offended

the lower middle class, the people who, though they had no
votes, formed the backbone of the National Guard. The republicans had until now always found the National Guard against
them. The republicans were, so had thought not only the
officers but the men of the National Guard, perpetual disturbers
of the peace. The ordinary citizens in the National Guard had
never had much affection for Louis-Philippe or any of his governments, though they had been willing to defend them against the
"rabble." But now that the moderate republicans were more
moderate than ever, now that they were among the best patriots
in France, now that they denounced the exclusion of the small
shopkeeper, the petty employee and the artisan from the franchise,
now that there had been no workers' insurrection for several
years, the men of the National Guard turned against the government. If they had not done so, the revolution of 1848 would
never have succeeded; and that they did so was largely owing to
the moderate republicans and the policy of their newspaper, Le
National. The Jacobins and their paper, La Réforme, disliked
and distrusted the new policy of the moderates. They accused
them of treachery to the republican cause. They remembered the
jealousies and quarrels that had tended to separate them even in
the early thirties. But they did not refuse to co-operate with them
for many purposes. The link between the two main groups of
republicans was not yet broken; it was not broken until after the
revolution. Meanwhile, it was strong enough to stand all the
strains put upon it.

The radicals, or republicans of La Réforme, as they were called
at the time, were not themselves revolutionaries. But they were
in touch with the revolutionaries. While they and the moderates
were friends, or at least not enemies, the legal and illegal oppo-
sitions to the régime, though their efforts were not concerted,
were still moving in the same direction. I have used the expression a "chain of friendship" to describe the relations between the
various opponents of Guizot. They were never allies; they were
never even a group of friends. They did not feel alike, think
alike or work together. Friendship was not a relation that bound
each to all but only each to some. That is why I used the simile
of a chain. For a little time, though long enough to destroy his
power, all the opponents of Guizot marched together. They did

so almost without knowing it, because a variety of sympathies and interests, which might at other times have kept them apart, happened to draw them together. The most important link in the chain, though not the strongest, was the one binding the radicals to the moderates. So long as it held, all the forces opposed to the régime pulled against it more strongly than against each other.

In politics, especially in a country where there are no large organised parties, you never know how strong or how weak you are. You can perhaps estimate your own strength and that of your friends, but you can't exactly foretell the reactions of other groups to any initiative you may take. The republicans had been bold, active, and growing in numbers in the early thirties, and yet the government had repeatedly got the better of them. In the forties, the republicans were more cautious and less hopeful. It took them a long time to learn that circumstances were changing in their favour; indeed, they never knew, until after the revolution, how quickly they had changed; and then they made the mistake of thinking the change as profound as it had been rapid.

The moderate republicans had in 1846 got as far as making an electoral alliance in Paris with the Gauche Dynastique. To secure the alliance, the moderates had even consented to accept the monarchy. The Jacobins denounced the alliance, but their denunciation could for the time being make little difference. They would have nothing to do, so they said, with the Gauche Dynastique, but the enemies of the men whose friendship they refused still continued to be their own enemies. Whatever opportunity for intervention might be created for the radicals by the now more effective struggle waged by the Gauche Dynastique would obviously be used against the government. The radicals might refuse co-operation but they could not, unless they were willing to do nothing, ensure that their behaviour would profit only themselves and not also the monarchist opposition. They were bound to take the renewed and more hopeful struggle seriously, knowing that, if the legal opposition were completely defeated, the republic and social reform would be further off than ever.

Meanwhile, France, rather later than other countries, was beginning to suffer from the great famine that affected a large part of Europe in the middle forties. Guizot, like most of the other statesmen of his day, did nothing to alleviate the sufferings caused by the famine. His opponents decided to exploit a situation which he seemed powerless to remedy. They had been impressed by the successful campaign waged against the Corn Laws in England. A similar attempt to mobilise opinion in France might be more dangerous, but they thought it worth making. If the government thought such a campaign might lead to revolution, they would perhaps be the more willing to make timely concessions. In the meantime, the Gauche Dynastique and their moderate republican allies would insist upon the legal and orderly character of their campaign.

The campaign was a great success. It consisted of a series of political banquets held in Paris and in the provinces. The first banquet was on July 9th, 1847. It has sometimes been suggested that the banquets were so successful that the government decided to forbid the last of them, and that it was this action that precipitated the revolution. The suggestion is not quite true. The revolution was precipitated because a banquet was forbidden, but the banquet in question was not sponsored by the organisers of the campaign. This may appear a small matter but it is in fact important. The campaign organised by the opposition was abandoned in December because it was too successful in one sense and in another not successful enough. The opposition had found it easy to excite the people against the government, but they had not frightened the government into making concessions. What if the people got so excited as to get out of hand before Guizot saw the danger into which his obstinacy was putting the country? The opposition were frightened by their own success. They did not want a victory that might unloose forces too strong for them to control.

The decision to hold another banquet in Paris was made not by the opposition leaders but by the officers of the twelfth legion of the National Guard, the legion recruited from the poorest of the twelve districts into which the capital was then divided. The committee that was to organise the banquet was elected on December 16th, and its secretary wrote, as required by law, to the authorities to ask permission to hold it. His request was refused. But because he had made it before consulting his colleagues, the committee as a whole decided to take no notice of the refusal.

They also decided that the banquet could not achieve its object, which was to force the government to yield to public opinion, unless the opposition deputies were invited to it. The first thing these deputies did was to persuade the committee to postpone the banquet until after February 13th, when they proposed to inter- pellate the government in the Chamber about the reasons for refusing the permission asked for. And on February 14th, after the government had given an unsatisfactory reply to the inter- pellation, the opposition deputies persuaded everyone concerned in the scheme to agree to the election of a new Banquet Com- mittee on which all the opposition parties should be represented. They then asked that the price of tickets to the banquet should be trebled, that it should be held outside the twelfth district of Paris, that only parliamentary electors should be allowed to attend, and that Ledru-Rollin, the leader of the radical republicans, should not be invited. They were not given all they asked for: the price of the tickets was only doubled and Ledru-Rollin was invited. But they had succeeded in quite altering the character of the banquet, in making it a much more respectable affair than it would otherwise have been.

When, on the afternoon of February 21st, the government definitely forbade the banquet, all the political leaders associated with it, including even Ledru-Rollin and Louis Blanc, prepared to submit. The total effect of the politicians' intervention was, therefore, that on the plea of giving the proposed banquet a "broader basis," they had changed its character, and also that they had decided on surrender as soon as it was clear that the govern- ment meant business. That was how matters stood in the late afternoon of February 21st, the eve of the revolution. None of the political leaders at liberty, not even the more extreme republicans, intended to use force. The real revolutionaries, men like Blanqui and Barbès, were still in prison. Guizot, seeing how quickly all the enemies he had heard of had abandoned the fight, might well believe he was safe. If he had ever thought them formidable, he could now reflect that he had only to look formidable himself to tame them. And yet, to do the republicans justice, it was revolu- tion they feared and not the man they had so freely insulted all over France.

Chapter Four

THE SECOND REPUBLIC

I. THE REVOLUTION

IT WAS once again the students who started a revolution. Some of them had met in the offices of the newspaper, *L'Avant-Garde*, to discuss the banquet that was exciting the whole of France. It was after midnight when they heard there was to be no banquet. They had hoped that the great event, so ardently longed for, was about to happen, and now they were to be cheated by other men's cowardice. The deception was more than they could bear. They were eager to show the courage that the politicians apparently lacked; and they decided that the next day, February 22nd, they would hold a demonstration. They had reason to believe that their example might stir up the workers to revolt.

And so next morning they met together on the Place du Panthéon, and waited there till about eleven o'clock, when they were 200 strong. They then set out for the Palais Bourbon, the meeting-place of the French lower chamber, going the long way round through the working-class districts of Paris. No attempt was made to stop them until they reached the Palais Bourbon, and by that time the marching crowd was too great for the municipal guards to control it. Even before the National Guard were called up at five o'clock in the evening, news of the insurrection had spread all over Paris and the workers were busy building their barricades. Only the legions in the wealthier districts of Paris responded to the government's call; but this the authorities did not notice at the time. Evening was fast drawing in. When the regular troops already in Paris quickly captured the first barricades, the government were certain that the revolt was already over and they withdrew the troops from the working-class districts. Should there be more disturbances the next day, the troops

63

and the National Guard could, they thought, easily put an end to them.

But when, on the morning of the next day, the National Guard were again called out, only the Cavalry Legion (recruited from the rich) and three of the twelve infantry legions appeared in full strength and willing to obey orders. The nine other legions also mustered in greater strength than the day before, but they soon gave vent to their irritation against the government. Three-quarters of the force on whose loyalty the régime principally depended, the force recruited from the middle classes in the capital, were proving disloyal. The government might perhaps have relied on the regular troops. But the regulars were the army of France, at best politically indifferent and at worst liable, as they had done in 1789, to fraternise with the classes most likely to disturb the government. The National Guard were the chosen, the specially created, instrument of bourgeois ascendancy and defence. The defection of three-quarters of them meant that the middle classes were no longer united, that the less well-to-do among them had turned against the government. As soon as the king heard of the disaffection of the nine poorer legions, he decided to dismiss Guizot and appoint a less inflexible minister, Molé, in his place.

The fall of Guizot immediately pacified the rebellious legions. But the Paris workers were not pacified. They continued their attacks on military barracks and their resistance to the troops. They were the inveterate enemies of the régime; and no decision that the king could take, short of abdication, was likely to satisfy them. They would always have grievances worth a fight; they could only be pacified if it were proved to them that they were in danger of isolation, that the forces against them were stronger than they could hope to defeat.

And, indeed, that evening, the evening of Wednesday, February 23rd, the workers were in danger of isolation. The National Guard were reunited in loyalty to the throne, and the republican leaders, moderate and radical, were biding their time. If the workers continued in insurrection for a day or two longer, all the irritation felt against the king would quickly disappear. Men would expect him once again, as he had done many years ago, to save France from the revolutionaries. Time was now the king's ally, and a little patience would soon make him master of the situation.

But that same evening there happened an accident that destroyed all the king's hopes. As demonstrators celebrating the fall of Guizot were moving along the Boulevard des Capucines, they came into collision with some troops. The incident might have passed off quietly enough, but someone, perhaps without wanting to, fired a shot. This shot led to cries of treachery, panic and, in the end, to a regular fusillade. Thirty-six persons were killed and about seventy wounded.

This disaster turned all the people who had lately been reconciled to the king once more against him. There were rumours that Guizot's dismissal had been a mere expedient to enable the authorities to gain time, that a general massacre of the insurgents was intended, that everyone who had caused offence would suffer for what he had done. In times of disorder there are two fears to which moderate men are liable: fear of reaction and fear of revolution. Many of them, when the insurrection begins, sympathise with the insurgents; their sympathy turns to anger only when, after the first concessions have been made, the insurgents are still unsatisfied and determined on violence. If the insurgents are struck down before this anger has grown strong, sympathy revives and with it the fear of reaction. This was what happened after the accident in the Boulevard des Capucines. The king had meant no harm. Even if he hoped one day to regain the power he had shared with Guizot, he was too sensible and too humane to suppose he could regain it by shooting down Guizot's enemies in the streets of Paris. But the accident had happened, and the general panic and frantic fear of reaction occasioned by it gave the revolutionaries their chance. That night they built barricades all over Paris, looted the gunsmiths' shops and even some of the barracks. By the Thursday morning the insurgents were well-provided, well-armed, and in good heart. Though not everyone in Paris loved them, all Paris hated the king. Did the man they had so long laughed at now dare to frighten them?

Louis Philippe, when he heard of the Capucines massacre and the reaction of Paris to it, decided to be conciliatory and yet firm. He dismissed Molé and appointed an even more liberal ministry under Thiers and Barrot. He also put Bugeaud, the conqueror of

F

Algeria, in command of the troops in Paris. He thought he still had the situation well in hand.

Bugeaud, fully confident of success, launched his offensive at five o'clock in the morning on Thursday, February 24th. His orders were to try to pacify the insurgents, to announce the appointment of the new ministry to them, and to resort to force only when conciliation had proved a failure. The king loved power but he also disliked force and bloodshed.

Bugeaud soon found he could not carry out his orders. The insurgent leaders and the officers of the National Guard were in no mood to listen to the king's reasons. Or, rather, they were willing to listen but not to be convinced. Everywhere, the conversations between the rebels and the king's officers were long drawn out. They were also, in most cases, polite conversations, and the longer they continued the more difficult it was to put an end to them. Meanwhile, the troops began to fraternise with the national guardsmen and the insurgents. They were soon so well disposed to each other that fighting between them was unthinkable. Bugeaud's officers could think of nothing better to do than to send for new instructions and to report on the situation; and when Bugeaud read their reports he knew that the troops under his command were no longer willing to shed blood. There had been some fighting on the Place de la Concorde and at the Chateau d'Eau[1], but it was the result of misunderstandings. These preliminary conversations, so difficult to put an end to, had persuaded the would-be combatants that they at least were all good fellows. The king and his advisers might be villains or they might not; it was a difference of opinion not worth a civil war. When the king heard that Bugeaud's offensive had failed, he abdicated in favour of his grandson, the Count of Paris.

By midday the insurgents were masters of Paris. The political leaders, who had kept in the background while the fighting had lasted, now set about organising the victory. It was only natural they should do so. They would have been useless on the barricades; and yet without their help the insurgents would not have known what to do with their victory. This was so obvious to them that they never even attempted to seize power; no one needed to tell them they were unfit to govern a country like France.

---

[1] Flaubert has described it in L'Education sentimentale.

As soon as it was realised that the political future of France was now being decided, there were three groups of men willing to take the initiative. First of all, there were the moderate republican leaders who had met in the offices of their great newspaper, *Le National*. In the early afternoon, they set about deciding who were to constitute the provisional government that was now inevitable. When their list was complete, copies of it were thrown out to the crowd waiting in the street below. They then amended their list according to what they believed might satisfy the crowd's wishes, as expressed by their cries of anger and applause. It was in this way that the name of Barrot, the leader of the Gauche Dynastique, was struck out of the list, and that of Ledru-Rollin included in it. When the crowd appeared satisfied, a messenger was sent to the Palais Bourbon to inform those of the chosen who were not already in the offices of *Le National* that they were now members of the government of France.

The Jacobins, or radical republicans, were busy preparing another list in the offices of their great newspaper, *La Réforme*. Their list, as a matter of fact, included most of the names chosen quite independently by *Le National*, but it also included two others, Louis Blanc and Albert. Louis Blanc was at that time the most famous socialist in France and Albert was a working man popular with his own class in Paris.

While the republicans of *Le National* and *La Réforme*, helped by the crowds below their windows, were choosing a government for France, the Chamber of Deputies had met and were discussing the situation created by the king's abdication. The majority of them would have preferred a regency and a government led by Thiers and Barrot. Thiers they could trust; he had put down the workers' insurrection at Lyon in 1834. Barrot, according to the ideas generally received among parliamentarians, was entitled to a share of power. He was the leader of the Gauche Dynastique by whom the campaign of banquets had originally been conceived. Now that it had ended with the fall of Guizot and the king's abdication, the leader of this dangerous opposition was entitled to his reward. Barrot was well known to the deputies; he stood at the edge of political respectability, and they thought everything to the left of him ruinous for France. But Barrot, as we have seen, was rejected by the crowd outside the office of *Le*

National; he was too far to the right even for the supporters of the moderate republicans.

The deputies were not allowed to decide the future of France. The insurgents invaded the Palais Bourbon, and soon made it clear that nothing less than a republic and a provisional government would satisfy them. They would have nothing to do with a ministry led by Thiers, the man who had outwitted the republicans in 1830, and fired on the workers in 1834. The deputies felt their impotence and began quietly to disperse. Ledru-Rollin then read out to the crowd the list prepared by *Le National* and invited them to follow him to the Town Hall to instal the new government.

By 1848 there were established precedents in France to guide men's actions after a successful revolution. The new provisional government must be proclaimed at the Town Hall and there make its first declaration to the people.

The men on the list prepared by *Le National* arrived at the Town Hall first. Then came the two men who were on *La Réforme's* list but not on *Le National's*. Their claim to take part in the government was contested by the first comers. But in the end there was a compromise. It was agreed that the two who came later were to act as secretaries of the Provisional Government and to have full consultative rights.[1] The crowd outside the Town Hall would not have tolerated their exclusion.

The Provisional Government was never a united body. It had to decide within a few hours of its coming to power, whether to proclaim a republic immediately or else first consult the nation. The point was not an academic one. To decide on an immediate proclamation was to prefer Paris, where the workers and Jacobins were powerful, to the rest of France. To decide to consult the nation first was to allow the provinces, if they were so inclined, to reject what the capital had done. The moderates were in favour of consulting the people. If the people were not consulted, what would become of the republicans' democratic principles? The radicals wanted the republic immediately proclaimed. What Paris decided, France would accept. Besides, it was the Parisians who had made the revolution; to refuse them

---

[1] Soon after, the two secretaries became full members of the Provisional Government.

what they most wanted was a useless provocation. The moderates of course were in the majority, but both parties to the discussion knew that the crowd outside were clamouring for the republic. In the end, there was found a formula that both parties could accept and so worded that it might not offend the crowd. It was proclaimed that "the Provisional Government desire a republic, provided it is ratified by the people, who will be immediately consulted." The crowd took this declaration for a proclamation of the republic and were satisfied.

I have described in some detail the events of only four days. I have wanted to make it quite clear what sort of a revolution happened in Paris during those four days. There are three truths about this revolution that ought more particularly to be remembered. None of the political leaders made it; they did no more than assume control of it after it had succeeded. Not one of them (until Blanqui was released and that was only after the fighting was over) was closely in touch with the men who actually manned the barricades. Secondly, the insurrection might never have become a revolution but for the accident in the Boulevard des Capucines, which threw the National Guard into the arms of the insurgents after the moderates had got what they wanted, the dismissal of Guizot. Thirdly, the Provisional Government were not allies brought together by their common aims; they were only men whose names had appeared on lists designed to please as many Parisians as possible. From the first, this government included two hostile parties: a majority who hoped that France would soon save them from the tyranny of Paris, and a minority determined that as many concessions as possible should be made to Paris before France had the opportunity to make her will known.

II. UNTIL THE JUNE INSURRECTION

The moderate republicans had a seven to four majority in the Provisional Government and they knew that the provinces greatly preferred them to their Jacobin colleagues. Yet they felt that, for the time being, their position was weak. Until France had spoken there could not be a sufficient excuse for refusing the demands of the Parisians. The moderates had therefore to make concessions to the workers. They allowed a Jacobin, Caussidière, to become Prefect of Police in Paris, and they were obliged to give the Ministry of the Interior to Ledru-Rollin. Since the Minister of the Interior alone had the right to call out the National Guard, this was a great concession. Caussidière hurriedly organised a special workers' police force to keep order in Paris. Apart from Ledru-Rollin and Caussidière, the Jacobins and more extreme republicans could rely on the political clubs that came into existence, or at least into the light of day, immediately after the revolution. The most vigorous of these clubs were all either Jacobin or revolutionary. There was the *Société Fraternelle Centrale*, presided over by Cabet, whose peaceful communism was still widely attractive to the workers of Paris. Then there was the *Club des Amis du Peuple*, dominated by Raspail, who used his great influence to restrain the workers from violence. But both Cabet and Raspail, though they rebuked the violent, denounced the selfishness and arrogance of the rich. If they did not preach revolution, they brought the wealthy into contempt. There were also two important revolutionary clubs, the *Société Républicaine Centrale*, popularly called the *Club Blanqui*, and the *Club de la Révolution*, whose chief orator was the Creole Barbès. These four clubs soon became the terrors of France, because the moderate republican and the reactionary newspapers published the most dreadful accounts of their activities. Three of the clubs supported the Jacobin minority of the Provisional Government, while Blanqui was still further to the left, anxious to destroy whatever might prevent the rebirth of France. These clubs were less terrible than they appeared to the timid. Their influence was confined to Paris. They were never able to create strong ties with societies like themselves emerging in the provincial towns. They never guided or inspired, as the Jacobins of 1792-4 had done, radical minorities all over France. In Paris alone were they formidable. There they could provoke insurrections that the moderates were at first powerless to suppress. The clubs might have been dangerous if a man like Robespierre or Marat had gained control over them. Luckily for the moderates, Blanqui, the ablest of the revolutionaries, was no more than a conspirator and an insurgent. Ledru-Rollin and Louis Blanc, the two members of the government most popular in Paris, did not know how to use the mob to terrify and punish their colleagues. Nor, to do them justice, did they want to know. They were more anxious to please the workers than to use them.[1]

The moderates made two important concessions to the radicals and the socialists. On February 25th, they agreed to publish a decree promising work to all citizens, and then, to give effect to their promise, they ordered the immediate establishment of National Workshops (*Ateliers Nationaux*). Three days later, on February 28th, they set up a commission whose business was to report on the conditions of the working class and suggest methods of improving them. This commission, on which workers' delegates also sat, met at the Luxembourg Palace, and is known to history as the Luxembourg Commission.

Both these concessions were more apparent than real. The Provisional Government was not obliged to adopt the suggestions of the commission. It had been established only because Louis Blanc had threatened to resign if nothing were done for the workers; and, so long as armed power was in the hands of the workers, it was important he should not resign. While he was a member of the Provisional Government, the workers might be kept quiet; if he were free to excite them, they would be unmanageable. The moderates hoped that the Luxembourg Commission would become a talking shop, where the socialists could deafen and disgrace each other without endangering the peace, where they could waste their energies and exercise their voices. In this way, while they remained as ineffective as ever, the innocent might be frightened by their extravagance.

The National Workshops were meant to prevent the workers' starving and to keep them out of mischief. They were not run by the Luxembourg Commission but by the Ministry of Public Works, where the minister, Marie, the most moderate of the moderates, had no intention of putting into practice the theories of Louis Blanc. There were never in fact any workshops. The workers merely got certificates from the local authorities declar-

---

[1] The Jacobins of 1848 were not at all like the great Jacobins of the first revolution. They were more virtuous and more amiable. They probably loved justice more than they hated their political enemies. They were neither ruthless nor treacherous. They were not even cynics, as were nearly all the great Jacobins in 1793, except Robespierre and St. Just. Except for their vanity, the Jacobins of 1848 were fitter to be philanthropists than revolutionaries.

ing that they were out of work. They then took these certificates to certain offices, where they were either directed to help build embankments, or to other work, or else were sent home with a franc apiece in their pockets. There was no more to it than either digging or getting the dole. The National Workshops were as unlike as they could be the Social Workshops advocated by Louis Blanc, workshops meant to be state-aided and efficient producers' co-operatives competing on favourable terms with the private capitalists.

Soon after the National Workshops were established, an engineer, Émile Thomas, persuaded Marie to adopt a scheme for organising the workers in semi-military fashion. The whole organisation was to be controlled by a central office, set up outside the working-class districts of Paris. The central office was to see to it that the workers were dispersed widely and given work not too near their homes. Émile Thomas was put in charge of the National Workshops and allowed to employ as his subordinates former students of the *École Centrale des Arts et Manufactures*. The Paris workers had long been in the habit of taking advice from their juniors, and it was hoped that these serious young engineers might undo the harm done by students of law.

The government never knew what they wanted to do with the National Workshops. Some of them, anxious to prove that socialism was a failure, wanted the workshops to be wasteful and inefficient. Others were more anxious to use them to keep the workers out of the way of the demagogues. Émile Thomas, himself a moderate republican, was the apostle of efficiency; he knew that the workshops were not socialist and he wanted the workers kept busy. But Marie did not give him the support he needed. In spite of all his efforts, the National Workshops were neither efficient nor popular. They did, however, for three months, until nearly the end of May, keep many workers out of politics. On March 17th, April 16th and May 15th, when the revolutionary clubs organised demonstrations to put pressure on the government, the ateliers workers were not involved; and when at last Thomas and his young engineers began to lose their influence over the workers, the military and police power at the disposal of the government was much greater than it had been in February. It can, I think, be said of the National Workshops, that, had they been run efficiently, there would have been no June insurrection; and also that, had they not existed, the revolutionaries might have made a successful bid for power before the government were strong enough to prevent them.

For the revolutionaries, following the example of the Jacobins and the Commune of 1793–4, whenever they wanted to intimidate the government, organised a demonstration that might easily have turned into a revolt. These demonstrations, sometimes supported by the Luxembourg Commission and in which the clubs took the leading part, mark, according to their success or failure, the shifts in the balance of power in Paris between the moderates and the republicans to the left of them. The demonstration of March 17th, for instance, was a victory for the left. It was meant to encourage the government to resist middle-class opposition to a scheme for making the National Guard more popular by allowing into it persons who were not able to arm and equip themselves. Or rather, it was meant to encourage the radicals in the government to insist on resistance to pressure which the moderates were only too willing to give in to. March 17th was a pyrrhic victory for the left. The government had no money to spare to equip the new legionaries, and in June, when the workers rose in revolt, the National Guard was almost as much a middle-class affair as it had been in February. Not until 1871 did the Parisian National Guard become proletarian.

The next trial of strength, the demonstration of April 16th, was a joint enterprise of the Luxembourg Commission and the clubs. The men who prepared it had apparently two purposes. They wanted to stimulate the government to do more for the workers, and they also wanted to induce them to postpone the elections. The revolutionaries knew that the elections would go against them; they wanted more time to strengthen their alliances, to extend their propaganda and to extort real concessions from the government. No doubt they knew that, however long the elections were postponed, they must remain a small minority. But they could hope to become a formidable minority; and they could also hope that, once real concessions were made to the workers, it would be difficult to take them away.

The demonstration of April 16th was a failure. Ledru-Rollin, the leader of the Jacobins, in his capacity as Minister of the Interior, called out the National Guard and prevented the demonstration from reaching the Town Hall, the seat of the Provisional Government. It was therefore the radical leader who gave the moderates their first victory over the clubs. Why was Ledru-Rollin so anxious to serve his rivals? Some historians of the left have said that, being a bourgeois, he, when it came to the point, threw in his lot with his own class. But only a few days earlier, Ledru-Rollin had himself contemplated a workers' insurrection to help turn the moderates out of the government. No one knew better than he did that a general election would give a vast majority to the moderates and conservatives. He had argued that, if there must be an insurrection to break the obstinacy of the moderates, it should come before the Constituent Assembly was elected and not afterwards. It would be impossible for men who for nearly twenty years had preached the gospel of universal suffrage to launch an insurrection against the elected representatives of the people. But there was no reason why the Provisional Government, the product of one insurrection, should not be transformed by another. These were the sentiments of Ledru-Rollin. Why then did he call out the National Guard against the demonstrators on April 16th? Perhaps because he lacked the nerve to take the risks that a new insurrection would involve. Perhaps also, and this may have weighed more with him, because he distrusted Blanqui and could not bring himself to do what might make Blanqui master of Paris. Whatever his motives, his action certainly put it out of the power of the Jacobins and revolutionaries so to entrench themselves behind real concessions made to the workers, that the moderates, when their overwhelming majority was at last made evident, would not dare to dislodge them. The Luxembourg Commission and the National Workshops were only apparent concessions made to the socialists; they were things of straw and would be blown away by the first wind of reaction.

The elections, held at the end of April, were indeed a triumph for the moderate republicans. Out of nine hundred seats, they got five hundred. The Jacobins got only a hundred, while the other three hundred went to persons who called themselves republicans, because everyone did so at the time, but were really

Orleanists or Legitimists. They formed what came to be known as the Party of Order, and, for convenience sake, we may call them conservatives. When the Constituent Assembly met on May 4th, it replaced the Provisional Government by an Executive Commission of five members, of whom four were moderates and the fifth was Ledru-Rollin. It was in this way that the radical leader was rewarded for his behaviour on April 16th.

The moderate republicans had done well at the elections because the revolution that gave them power was still only two months old. They had the prestige of success, and they were the most conservative of all the heirs of that revolution. They were doing their best, as the French people well knew, to prevent the radicals and revolutionaries from seizing power; and they were now supported by the church. The church had had enough of bankrupt allies; she had placed her great credit at the disposal first of the ultra-royalists and then of the Orleanists, and had found both branches of the old dynasty unexpectedly weak. She now had to look for other allies, stronger and more popular; and for a few weeks she thought she could find them in the moderate republicans. Her decision was all the easier because the Catholic Party, led by Montalembert, had already persuaded many good Christians that devotion to the church was compatible with acceptance of at least some of the principles inherited from the great revolution. The Pope had long ago declared Lamennais a heretic, but it was to his influence, though the clergy would never have admitted it, that the moderate republicans now owed the support of the church. He it was who had first taught men that the church might come to terms with the revolution. Gregory XVI had condemned him in 1834 and his Catholic associates had dutifully abandoned him. But it was not long before they had again begun to preach his principles, more cautiously and with less fervour, giving up the part of them that had given most offence at Rome, the doctrine that church and state should be separate. And this time the Pope had not interfered. Montalembert and the chastened Catholic Party, though they had not denied popular rights, had condemned insurrection; and, though they had praised every liberty, had used their best arguments to defend the rights of private education and association, the two liberal principles most useful to the church. They had not been republicans, but they had, in fourteen years, succeeded in persuading not a few good Catholics that the cause of reaction was not always the cause of the church. In April 1848, it seemed to many people that they were right. This new mood of the church was not to last long, but while it lasted it helped to make almost all the respectable classes well-disposed towards the moderate republicans. Hence their great electoral triumph in April, when even the conservatives thought it politic to call themselves republicans.

The election of the Constituent Assembly was a great blow to the extreme left. Instead of accepting the inevitable, they tried to impose their will on the nation by force. On May 15th they prepared another demonstration. Their ostensible purpose was to petition the Assembly to intervene against the Russians in favour of the Poles. The Assembly had passed a resolution forbidding the direct presentation of public petitions by large bodies of people. The demonstrators decided to ignore this resolution. Led by the revolutionaries from the clubs, they invaded the Assembly, dissolved it and drew up the list of a new provisional government to consist only of extreme radicals and revolutionaries. They then, according to tradition, marched to the Town Hall to proclaim the new government; but on their way they met the National Guard who blocked their path and dispersed them. The leaders of the insurrection, Blanqui and Barbès, were arrested; and Caussidière, the Jacobin Prefect of Police, though nothing could be proved against him, was obliged to resign his post. For the first time since February preponderant force in Paris was in the hands of the government.

May 15th, for which Blanqui must take the blame, was a serious mistake. All the good will that France had felt for the workers of Paris, who had borne the brunt of a revolution which had become popular after it had succeeded, was at once dissipated. The "reds," as they were now called, had tried to establish a dictatorship and to destroy a popular Assembly. They had endangered and insulted France. It was high time, so many good and timid people began to think, to put an end to their plots.

After May 15th, the moderates believed that the country was fast becoming so frightened and annoyed by the socialists and revolutionaries that it would excuse whatever measures might be taken against them. They decided to put an end to the National

Workshops. Socialist historians have sometimes suggested that the moderates, when they decided to abolish the workshops, hoped to sting the workers into revolt, that they might then destroy militant socialism by force of arms. Nobody claims to see further into the minds of people they dislike than these socialist historians. But those of us who must rely on mere evidence have to be more cautious. The moderates knew that the abolition of the workshops might lead to a revolt. There is no reason to believe they hoped it would do so. The workshops had been imposed upon them by the radicals and socialists;[1] they were notoriously expensive and inefficient, and now that the moderates were powerful, they were determined to suppress what they had always thought an abuse. Émile Thomas warned the government that abolition would precipitate a revolt. His warnings were not without their effect. Although he was dismissed on May 26th, the final decision to abolish the workshops was not taken till June 21st, when a decree was published ordering all the workers belonging to them either to join the army, if they were under 25 years of age, or else to hold themselves in readiness to go to the provinces to work there. When a workers' deputation visited Marie, the Minister of Public Works, he told them that the decree must be obeyed and that it would, if necessary, be enforced. The next day, June 23rd, Falloux, when he proposed the abolition of the workshops within three days, also proposed that some of the workers should receive one franc a day for another three months and that an indemnity of three million francs should be paid to the others. And when at last the revolt broke out, the Assembly decided that the workers not involved in it must be paid as before, so that as many of them as possible might have a motive for refraining from violence.

The workers set about building their barricades on the evening of June 22nd, but they were not attacked until next day. This delay is the only serious evidence that the authorities wanted the insurrection to spread until it was large enough to enable them to strike a heavy and mortal blow at militant socialism. But the delay, if we take notice of what the government did in other ways to appease the workers, can be more credibly explained. The

---

[1] The workshops actually set up were not at all what the socialists wanted. But they were a concession made to them, the best that could be got out of the moderates.

police and the military authorities believed that the February revolution had succeeded because the troops had attacked the barricades piecemeal, as they were put up, and so had been dispersed and made incapable of the combined and encircling attack that could alone make suppression effective. The best policy, they now perhaps thought, was to try to buy off as many workers as possible and then make sure that those who insisted on fighting were thoroughly beaten.

The June insurrection, the second greatest workers' revolt of the nineteenth century, lasted three days. The fighting was bitter, and several thousand persons lost their lives. The National Guard fought with a will against the workers; the February alliance between the proletariat and the lower middle class was now at an end. None of the well-known Jacobin, socialist or revolutionary leaders was involved in the insurrection. Blanqui and Barbès were in prison; Ledru-Rollin, Louis Blanc and their friends had nothing whatever to do with it. The moderates and conservatives would have been only too pleased to prove something against them, had they been able. The revolt, as far as the police authorities knew, was leaderless; it was an explosion of anger directed against the new rulers of France. What the workers hoped to gain by it, it is impossible to say.

The failure of the June insurrection had important repercussions, not only in France, but abroad. All over Europe it gave courage to the counter-revolutionaries. In provincial France, it provoked the greatest "red scare" since the first revolution. Squads of indignant bourgeois and peasants armed with sticks searched the woods and forests for revolutionaries. Everywhere respectable citizens were determined that there should be an adequate revenge.

III. THE CONSERVATIVES TAKE OVER (JUNE 1848—JUNE 1849)

The abortive *coup d'état* of May 15th and the June insurrection destroyed the always precarious alliance between the moderate republicans, on the one hand, and the Jacobins, social reformers and revolutionaries on the other. The revolutionaries were broken and dispersed; they were either in prison, abroad or in hiding. Being weak, they had acted on May 15th as if they were strong; they had tried to terrify and to dominate France and had only made her anxious, vindictive and unreasonable. And then, after Blanqui's bid for power, came the workers' insurrection. France had never been more persuadable and gentle than in February, when she had awoken as if to a new day, not knowing what it would bring, but full of hope. At that time even the church had seemed to believe in progress. Since then four months had scarcely passed and everything was changed. For this change the republicans were alone responsible; they had had the political stage entirely to themselves. They had quarrelled and even killed each other. From now onwards, new actors were to crowd onto the stage until all the republicans were at last driven off it.

It looked, at the end of June 1848, as if the revolutionaries were put down, the radicals pushed to one side and the moderates triumphant. During the June days, the Executive Commission was suspended and absolute power during the emergency given to Eugène Cavaignac, a moderate republican. When the emergency was over, the Executive Commission was not restored; Cavaignac resigned the dictatorship but was made Chief of the Executive, to serve until the new Constitution of France was ready. He ruled France for six months, until the election of Louis Bonaparte to the presidency. His ministers were all moderate republicans.

But power was already moving away from the republicans. The church had abandoned them. The Constituent Assembly, elected before the Blanquist *coup* of May 15th and the June insurrection, no longer reflected the popular mood. France was already much less republican than the deputies she had so lately elected. And these deputies were themselves moving to the right. When the Assembly first met, it was a predominantly republican body and the conservatives in it were disposed to let the republicans take the lead. Since the June days a considerable number of moderate republicans had passed over to the conservatives, to the *Parti de l'Ordre*. Now, the conservatives, though they had kept their principles very much up their sleeves during the recent election, were not democrats. They did not believe in universal suffrage nor even in the mildest social reform. They were just royalists, mostly Orleanists, men of property who had decided to make the best of the republic they thought inevitable. Before the June days it had not been possible for them to take the initiative, but now they were more self-confident. They left the responsible posts to the moderate republican leaders and pushed them towards reaction as fast as their uneasy but still animate loyalty to republican principles would let them go.

It was therefore the moderates, well supported by the conservatives, who were responsible for the first reactionary laws. The decree of July 28th, 1848, destroyed the autonomy of the clubs; it forbade secret societies; it enacted that political meetings not open to the public could not be held except with the permission of the authorities; and it obliged the clubs to open their doors to the public, to allow the presence of a police official, to keep a full record of all discussions and resolutions and to forbid any proposal contrary to public order and morals. When the decree was debated in the Assembly, it was made clear that public order involved the maintenance of the family and of private property. Two laws made in August established a new régime for the press. Newspaper editors were once again obliged to pay caution-money, while insults against the Assembly and the republic, as well as attacks on the family and private property, were made press offences. As only the highest administrative officials had lost their posts after the February revolution, these laws were enforced by persons who were even more conservative than the men who made them. The radicals, the socialists and the revolutionaries were deprived of their most effective political instruments.

The moderate republicans were bound to grow weaker as soon as the peasants and the men of property turned against the revolution. They had been popular at first because their moderation and respectability had seemed to guarantee the good behaviour of their allies to the left. As soon as the ineptitude of the moderates, the indecision of the Jacobins, and the reckless tactics of the revolutionaries had plunged Paris into civil war, it was inevitable that both extremes should gain ground at the expense of the middle party. But there are other reasons that explain the weakness of the moderates. In March the Provisional Government had published a decree increasing all direct taxes by 45 centimes in the franc. This most unpopular decree had come too late to affect the voting in the April elections, but later on, when the increased taxes began to be levied, it was the moderate republicans who bore the full brunt of popular resentment. What had the republic brought to France? Civil war in Paris and a 45 per cent increase in direct taxation! The conservatives could well afford to deal firmly with such discredited men as the republicans.

Besides, the moderate republicans had no leader. Cavaignac was honest. But he was not as clever as Thiers, who led the *Parti de l'Ordre*; nor had he the demagogic appeal of Ledru-Rollin. He infuriated the radicals by making so many concessions to the conservatives, and yet failed to win the latter's confidence. They would tolerate him while they could use him, but when the time came to go further than any republican could follow, they would throw him aside.

What made the moderates weak gave strength to the Jacobins. Their leaders had done nothing to help the Blanquists on May 15th or the workers during the June insurrection; and on April 16th Ledru-Rollin had even used force to defend the government against the clubs. The revolutionaries and the workers had little cause to be grateful to him. And yet it was to him that the left rallied as soon as the reaction began. He had neither taken part in nor condoned the repression of the workers. He had tried to prevent violence, and he had protested against the punitive measures adopted by the Assembly. Of his sympathy for the workers there could be no doubt, and after the June days he was the most important man left in France still willing and able to speak out on their behalf. Besides, he was resolutely opposed to the conservatives. He could not prevent reaction, but he could and did promote so formidable a resistance to the reactionaries that it converted large sections of the French people to republicanism and social reform. In March and April 1848, vast numbers of Frenchmen were well-disposed to the republican cause; but they knew nothing of it and soon deserted it. Those who joined the Jacobins after June 1848 were converted in a quite different fashion; they were stalwarts who had learned to hate the enemies of the republic. Adversity taught the Jacobins and socialists, uneasy allies before June, that they must work more closely together. Their alliance was sealed at a banquet held on September 22nd. There were still four socialists active in the

G

Constituent Assembly—Victor Considérant, the Fourierist, Pierre Leroux, formerly a member of the Saint-Simon sect, Louis Blanc and Proudhon. It is therefore not a paradox, but a simple and important truth, that in December 1851, when Louis Bonaparte destroyed the second republic, there were many more true republicans in France than ever before. The most fruitful and perhaps also the noblest year of Ledru-Rollin's life began after June 1848, when he started the fight against a reactionary movement that was too strong for him.

The three and a half years from June 1848 to December 1851 cover a number of stages on the road to Cæsarism. During the first stage, from June until the election of Louis Bonaparte as President of France, the moderate republicans and the conservatives made the clubs harmless and bridled the press; during the second stage, the conservatives and the President worked together to destroy the Jacobins; during the third stage, the President and the conservatives, while they still persecuted the Jacobins, gradually became enemies, until at last, on December 2nd, 1851, Louis Napoleon made himself sole master of France. The revolutionaries, the Jacobins and the conservatives were all either destroyed or outwitted; only the moderates, so much the strongest party immediately after the revolution, lapsed quietly into insignificance.

The moderate republicans, had they known how, could perhaps have saved themselves and the mild revolution they stood for. They might have run the national workshops efficiently and so reconciled the bourgeois and the peasants to them. By so doing they would have weakened the influence of the revolutionaries and Jacobins in Paris. They might have repealed the 45-centimes tax when they saw it was so unpopular as to be impossible to collect. They might have made a different constitution and so prevented the easy triumph of Louis Napoleon. They had the majority in the Constituent Assembly, and some of them knew that the direct election of the President might be dangerous. And yet, though de Tocqueville, in the committee formed to draft the constitution, had repeatedly warned them of the danger, they allowed a narrow majority of that committee to carry the proposal that the president should be directly elected by the people.

The election of Louis Napoleon was announced on December

20th, 1848. He got three-quarters of the votes cast, Cavaignac less than a fifth; Ledru-Rollin got only one-twentieth, but then no one had expected him to get more. It was the total defeat of Cavaignac, the "saviour" of France, who had put down the June insurrection, that was astonishing. The moderates were still numerous in the Assembly, but Cavaignac's defeat virtually deprived them of power. At the elections to the next legislature, elections that were to take place as soon as the Constituent Assembly had completed its task, they must expect to lose most of their seats. The conservatives, on the other hand, were full of confidence. They had supported the candidature of Louis Napoleon. If some of them doubted the wisdom of this policy they were soon reassured by Thiers. The great Napoleon's nephew, he said, was not at all like his uncle; he was even rather stupid. Thiers was sure he could manage him, and it was clever politics to use the prestige of a Bonaparte to dish the republicans. In return for their support, Louis Napoleon promised the conservatives that, if he were elected, he would retain the laws against the clubs, keep fifty thousand troops in Paris, refuse to recognise the Frankfurt Parliament and support the King of Sardinia against the Italian republicans. Thiers thought the bargain an excellent one. How could a man be dangerous who had twice made a fool of himself, who was living on borrowed money, who had only a few personal supporters and one or two newspapers working for him? In the drawing-rooms of Paris Louis Napoleon appeared insignificant. He was not a general, he was not a revolutionary, he had lived abroad for years; an experienced politician like Thiers might well feel that he was more than a match for the dullest and most silent of Bonapartes. Louis Napoleon triumphed at the polls because both the peasants and the more substantial bourgeois voted for him; he was also supported by not a few radicals and revolutionaries who would not waste on Ledru-Rollin or Raspail votes that could be used to keep Cavaignac out of power.

As soon as Louis Napoleon became president, he got rid of the moderate republican ministry and substituted a conservative one for it. His first prime minister was Odilon Barrot, but the real power behind the government belonged to Thiers. The President and his ministers now worked hard to put an end to the

Constituent Assembly. They could not govern France at their ease through a parliament still predominantly republican, however timid it might be. Though the Assembly had a legislative programme that would require another year to be completed, it took the government only five months to frighten it into dissolving itself. Though France was officially a republic, the government treated every republican demonstration as an attack upon itself. It did whatever it could to discredit the régime still approved by the majority of the Assembly. It could do so the more easily because the civil service and the police owed obedience only to the President and his ministers.

In Cavaignac's time, the Assembly had voted credits for an expeditionary force to be sent to Italy to help Piedmont against the Austrians. The new government ordered this force to march on Rome to restore the Pope to his throne. The order was illegal, but when the Assembly protested its protests were ignored. There was nothing the Assembly could do to force the government to take notice of its protests. The contempt with which they were treated humiliated and frightened the deputies. Since the presidential election, they could not doubt they were unpopular with the nation. Prudence and dignity seemed to require that the Assembly should not engage in a struggle that could only expose it to ridicule. As soon as it had voted the budget, it hastened to dissolve itself. Better death than dishonour, especially as that death was only political.

The elections for the Legislative Assembly gave a large majority to the conservatives. But what impressed France much more than this victory was the large radical vote. Of 750 seats the conservatives got 450 and the Jacobins 180. This was astonishing enough, but it was yet more astonishing that three persons voted radical for every five that voted conservative. The Jacobins had never had so many supporters in France before. It may be that many of them voted radical not because they liked radicalism but because they feared Louis Napoleon and Thiers. Whatever their motives, they had voted radical when the radical cause was in danger; they were friends of the democratic republic (for republicanism in France meant democracy), and they were not fair weather friends.

The result of the elections was therefore not a conservative triumph but a "red" scare.[1] The Jacobins had carried not only Paris and many of the larger towns (except in the west and north); they had also for the first time gained successes in rural areas. It was only a beginning, but that there should be such a beginning was itself enough to frighten men of property. What would happen to France if even the peasants were not immune from infection? In the army, too, there had been support for the radicals. A disease that had been confined to certain parts of the country was now spreading everywhere, corrupting classes and institutions on whose health and docility men of property had always felt they could depend. The conservatives were not perhaps as frightened as they had been during the June days, but they were as deeply disturbed.

As soon as the Legislative Assembly met, the Jacobins launched their attack. On June 11th, Ledru-Rollin interpellated the government on Oudinot's expedition to Rome. He declared it unconstitutional because one of the clauses of the constitution read that "the Republic respects all foreign nations and never uses its forces against the liberties of any people." The Assembly supported the government against the Jacobins. On June 13th several radical newspapers published a manifesto declaring that the President and the ministers had violated the constitution and that the National Guard were rising against them. The manifesto called upon the troops to defend the constitution. That same day, Ledru-Rollin and the officers of three legions of the National Guard organised a demonstration against the Rome expedition. The demonstrators were charged by cavalry and easily dispersed. Ledru-Rollin and several other Jacobin and socialist leaders fled abroad.

IV. THE PRESIDENT AGAINST THE CONSERVATIVES

The demonstration of June 13th, 1849, has often been called a mistake. It was so complete a failure that it made its sponsors look

[1] It was the second "red" scare. It was "red" because, since the February revolution, it had become fashionable in conservative circles to call the radicals "reds." On February 24th, 1848, the crowd outside the Town Hall in Paris had wanted the red flag for the new republic, but Lamartine, a moderate republican, had saved the tricolor for France. The red flag was at that time not socialist but insurrectionary. It was the flag of revolutionary and radical Paris. Lamartine had persuaded the crowd that only the tricolor was acceptable to France.

ridiculous. And it was not even what it purported to be; most of
the radical leaders whose names appeared on the Manifesto afterwards proved they had never signed it. The bolder spirits had
once again taken matters into their own hands and had miscalculated the probable consequences. The authorities now had
the excuse they wanted to make repression more severe. But
the folly of the Jacobins was not without excuse; the government
and the Assembly were doing what the constitution forbade. What
else could the Jacobins do to prevent the violation of the republican constitution, knowing, as they did, that, the constitution
once destroyed, there could be no hope of power or influence for
them? Many soldiers had voted radical, especially in Paris; that,
too, encouraged the Jacobins to act. The Manifesto, bearing
false signatures, was surely a mistake; but the demonstration was
perhaps the least the Jacobins could do under the circumstances.[1]

The repression that followed June 13th did less harm to the
republican cause than anyone, even the republicans, knew at the
time. And yet at the time it seemed severe. The three legions
involved in the demonstration were suppressed, soldiers and non-
commissioned officers suspected of radical sympathies were
transferred to Algerian regiments; and on June 13th a state of
siege was proclaimed in Paris and the eleven departments closest
to the capital. Two days later, the state of siege was extended to
the five departments near Lyon. At the same time there was
passed a law granting to military authorities, as soon as a state of
siege was proclaimed, all the powers belonging to the civil
government. The Assembly hoped this law would make repression easier by depriving accused persons of their usual rights.
They did not notice how strong a weapon they were placing in
the President's hand. Should he ever want to make a *coup d'état*,
some of the great obstacles in his way were already removed.
There were also other repressive measures. The law of June
19th, 1849, allowed the government, at their own discretion, to
suppress any political club. This law was made for only one year,

---

[1] The Jacobins never preached insurrection against a legal government. They had
abstained from violence in February, on May 15th and in June 1848. But they
believed in using force in defence of the constitution. What is more, though they
never advised violence against a legal government, they did not mind being called
revolutionaries. They gloried in the name of Robespierre though they never
followed his example.

but it was renewed until after the *coup d'état*, when Article 291 of the Penal Code and the Law of Associations of 1834 were revived. The law of July 27th made it an offence for any newspaper to insult the President or to attempt to turn soldiers from their obedience; and the courts interpreted both these offences in the widest sense. The prefects were ordered to "purify" the teaching profession. The village schoolmaster, in France as in many Continental countries, was already the most active recruiting agent for the radical cause. It was he who was teaching the peasants to take an interest in matters that had never concerned them before.

From June 1849 until December 1851, when Louis Napoleon made his *coup d'état*, there were two major political conflicts in France. There was the conflict between the conservatives and the President, a conflict for power between the men who had hoped to manage Napoleon and the man who had proved too clever for them; and there was also the conflict, more important but less spectacular, between the bureaucracy, loyal to property and privilege, and the republicans. The most active republicans were now all Jacobins,[1] and to the police they appeared enemies of property. The President and the conservatives, though they were open rivals, were united in their fear of the radicals.

Once again, as in earlier periods of repression, the only republicans tolerated by the police were the moderates. Their newspapers, *Le National*, *Le Siècle* and *La Presse*, still circulated freely, though they were bought in smaller numbers—a natural consequence of the decreased importance of the moderates. But the Jacobins and socialists were struck at without mercy. Every sort of association that might be useful to them was either persecuted or rigidly controlled. A political meeting called for a special occasion might, if the police felt so inclined, be treated as an unauthorised club, making those who organised and attended it liable to all the penalties against secret societies. Workers' Friendly Societies that gave money or other help to strikers were also treated as unauthorised political clubs and therefore as secret societies. If a Friendly Society did not take

[1] That is to say, all the republicans to the left of the moderates now worked together. The socialists knew that the defence of the republic must now take precedence over everything, and in that defence the Jacobins quite naturally took the first place.

advantage of a permission granted by law to seek government protection, it was supposed by the police and the courts that it must be engaged in political activities and therefore an unauthorised club. Workers' co-operatives sometimes annoyed the police only because they made a profit, and their shareholders' meetings were thought dangerous to the public. The police, in their attitude to the workers and republicans, were simple and consistent. Whatever brought workers together, except under the roofs of their employers, must, they thought, be a threat to peace and property. Such meetings, except in Paris, Lyon and a few other places, had scarcely ever happened before 1848. They were an innovation of the second republic, and they were a dangerous innovation. Had there not been a civil war in Paris and disturbances all over the country? The police had had trouble with the republicans long before 1848. But they had for years kept them in their place. And then, in February 1848, an accident had converted a perpetual but limited nuisance into an overwhelming danger for France. The police were determined, even if they could not destroy it, to reduce radicalism to its old proportions. For them it was merely a problem of making society once again manageable. They knew nothing about the social causes of the disorders it was their business to suppress. They were glad to find themselves supported once more by a strong government.

After June 1849 the authorities launched a sustained attack against the Jacobin and socialist press. *La Réforme* was soon killed by judicial fines. Proudhon's *Représentant du Peuple*, founded in November 1848, died of financial exhaustion after it had accumulated fines amounting to 81,000 francs. Proudhon's paper lasted less than a year, but it was easily the greatest socialist newspaper of the second republic.

I must interrupt my story at this point to say something more about Proudhon. He had made a reputation even before 1848. He had already made a friend and then an enemy of a man, younger and less well-known than himself, but destined to become more famous. Proudhon's reputation outside France is perhaps smaller than it might be because Marx attacked him so often and so violently. Already in 1840, when Marx was only 22, Proudhon had published his *What is Property?* In 1846 Marx, before his quarrel with Proudhon, had praised him for showing how the institution of private property had distorted all economic relations between men. He had called his work "the scientific manifesto of the French proletariat"; he had treated him as the first scientific socialist. Whether Proudhon was scientific in any sense in which earlier socialists were not, I cannot say. But he was certainly a new kind of socialist, harder and shrewder than the others. He had denounced the sentimental rhetoric of the radicals, their senseless imitation of the first Jacobins. He was by birth a peasant, self-educated and self-reliant, at once conceited and self-critical, anxious to please no one except his friends, and yet a generous enemy. Before June 1848, while the workers could still hope that the promises made to them would be kept, they preferred to listen to Cabet and Louis Blanc; or, if they felt aggressive, they could learn from Blanqui that only a little courage would destroy the system that oppressed them. But Blanqui was now in prison and the clubs quite discredited. In their present mood, bitter and disillusioned, the workers turned to Proudhon. He had attacked the leaders they no longer trusted, he made them no easy promises and he was obstinate in their defence. His courage and independence comforted them. Proudhon was a man of the people, the only great socialist leader of his century who was one.

Proudhon has been accused of many inconsistencies. He was wrong, so his critics have often said, and Marx was right. It may be so, but a man's influence does not depend on the strength of his logic. The French workers, after the June disaster, were in a mood to listen to home truths. Proudhon's roughness and cynicism suited them; and behind his manner they could sense the hatred of injustice, the contempt for power, the obstinate resolve never to be flattered or conciliated, the conviction that, however great the disaster, the fight must be renewed, though by other means—all the emotions and beliefs (and there were others less good) that lay at the heart of the French working-class revolutionary movement. Proudhon warned the workers that the struggle for equality was a hard struggle, that the odds were at present against them, that the time for rhetoric and comedy was past, that there was much more to politics than just violence. If he had had the most beautiful and consistent theory to offer them, he could not have spoken more to the purpose of their feelings.

He denounced the state as a social organisation naturally repressive, he denounced private capitalism, he praised workers' co-operatives, he taught that only the small community can be just, that property must not be abolished but made universal. By rejecting communism, he appealed to one of the strongest passions of the French worker, the ambition to be his own master. His unsuccessful attempts to reconcile his individualism with the economic facts did not interest the workers. He wanted what they wanted and that was enough for them. It was easy, since June 1848, to persuade the workers that the state was their enemy and the instrument of their oppressors; and in those days, when most of them worked in small workshops, it was natural that the ambition to be their own masters should still be strong. It was not until the turn of the century, when repeated free elections and the emergence of organised parties made the capture of the state seem more possible, when large-scale production was more common in France, when the trade unions were numerous and strong, that the French socialist movement at last became predominantly Marxist. But the thirty years after 1848 belonged to Proudhon; and if he had a serious rival, that rival was Blanqui, not Marx. Proudhon sat in the Constituent Assembly; in it he considered himself, especially after the June insurrection, a representative of the proletariat in a bourgeois assembly, and he behaved accordingly. His attacks on Louis Napoleon led to his arrest and imprisonment in June 1849, and he was not set free until three years later. His imprisonment was not severe and he was able to keep in touch with his friends.

Proudhon's influence was confined to the urban workers. His ascendancy was restricted to the socialist, and therefore smaller, part of the republican movement. But the Jacobins gained adherents in districts where no socialist would have been listened to. In southern, eastern and central France there was organised a vast network of secret societies, some of them altogether submerged and others disguised as charitable institutions. These societies were affiliated to one another and communicated through secret agents. They were directed by central committees established in Paris and Lyon.[1] Most of their members were armed. They were armed not to make a revolution but to prevent a *coup*

---

[1] Some were even in touch with the radical émigrés in London.

d'état. They were making such progress, even in the rural areas, that they could, for the first time in their history, hope for an electoral victory in the not too distant future; and they were determined, should they gain such a victory, not to allow Louis Napoleon to deprive them of its fruits. They worked quietly and hopefully, trying to remain unnoticed by the police. From the middle of 1850 they even refrained from contesting by-elections, lest small and premature victories should alarm their enemies. They were preparing a surprise for France at the next general election.

Meanwhile the President and the conservatives were trying to deprive each other of power. The Barrot Ministry, docile to Thiers, had treated the President almost with contempt. Louis Napoleon had been timid and silent, and therefore disregarded; but he chose his quarrel with his ministers cleverly. He asked for an amnesty for the men punished after the June insurrection. Barrot refused. And then Louis Napoleon got more popularity at an even cheaper price; though he knew he could do nothing to prevent it, he protested against the Pope's reactionary policy after the French had restored Rome to him. But the conservatives approved that policy. When, therefore, Napoleon dismissed Barrot, it looked as if humanity and the republic had won a little victory.

It was on October 31st, 1849, that Louis Napoleon dismissed the Barrot Ministry and replaced it by another chosen among his own supporters. The new ministry did not enjoy the confidence of the Assembly, but the conservatives could not afford to protest too strongly. France was no longer a parliamentary monarchy, and Louis Napoleon was as much the representative of the people as was the conservative majority in the Assembly. Indeed, he was the more representative of the two, for he had polled three-quarters of the votes cast and they scarcely more than a half. The French people cared nothing for parliamentary government; they had voted for the conservatives in May 1849 for exactly the same reason as for Louis Napoleon in the previous December; they had voted because they were afraid of the "reds"; and if the "reds" were to be kept in order, this was a task better done by one man than by several hundreds. The conservatives were not even united; some of them were Legitimists, others were Orleanists, and still others Catholics and nothing more. The Catholics were quite willing to sacrifice the principles of parliamentary government if they could make good terms for the church with the President. Napoleon could profit from divisions between the conservatives just as the republicans were to do in the early seventies. In this contest for power with Thiers, Napoleon had one great advantage; he was free to buy support where he could find it and had no need to hold together a precarious alliance.

The conservatives continued to make themselves unpopular. In March 1850, having discussed it for many months, they passed one of the most famous of modern French laws, the *Loi Falloux*, which abolished the state's monopoly of education, and therefore undid one of the great achievements of the first revolution. It allowed anyone with a bachelor's degree to open a primary school. The law was ostensibly intended to free education from the exclusive control of the state, but, as its sponsors and everyone else knew, it was made for the benefit of the church. The church alone was rich enough to open many schools, and the church controlled her schools not less severely than the state. While the church schools were made free of the state, the state schools were not left free of the church. The new law put them under the control of a variety of committees and councils on which the clergy were well represented.[1] The *Loi Falloux* did not make education much freer than it had been; it rather divided it into two kinds, state and clerical; and really private schools remained almost as rare as they had been. The new law irritated many respectable people who had no love for the republicans and were in no way hostile to religion but were anxious that the church should not be more powerful. Only a few years before, most of the Orleanists who now voted for the *Loi Falloux* had themselves been anti-clerical. They had changed their minds since 1848 and were now willing to make large concessions to the church in the hope that her control of education might put young men's minds out of reach of radical and socialist propaganda. Even Thiers, who was more uneasy about the law than the other Orleanists, agreed that primary education should be controlled by the

[1] As a matter of fact the clergy were never able to interfere effectively with the state schools. But it looked at the time as if the *Loi Falloux* would enable them to do so.

church, because religion is good for the lower classes. But he did not want the church to control secondary schools, attended in those days only by children of the well-to-do. Thiers also spoke against free and obligatory primary education. The *Loi Falloux* was possible because the upper middle class were at last growing reconciled with the church that Voltaire had ridiculed for their benefit. The rich had begun to notice that the priest was their friend and the village schoolmaster their enemy.

This change of heart was not sudden. Already, during the July Monarchy, attempts had been made to conciliate the church. The law of June 28th, 1833, had given the clergy extensive control of primary schools. While Guizot was in power it was twice proposed to allow the opening of private secondary schools. But both projects, Villemain's in 1841 and Salvandy's in 1847, had failed. The Catholics were not satisfied with the concessions made to them, while the liberals and moderate republicans thought them excessive. The value of the church as an organ of moral discipline was not denied, but in spite of the good will of Guizot and the king, the pretensions of the Catholics had irritated the bourgeois and made them suspicious. There had still been a gap between the least that the church would take and the most the bourgeois state would offer. This gap was closed during the second republic, when the well-to-do, now more frightened than they had ever been, were willing to make greater concessions.

The *Loi Falloux* was not liked except by the conservatives who made it. Its sponsors, all but the pious among them who had acted for the sake of the church, had hoped to strike at the radicals and the enemies of property. But their action was not so interpreted by everyone. Many humble and respectable people, friendly to religion but suspicious of anything that increased the power of the church, did not like the law. The church, no doubt, was almost as necessary to society as the religion she preached; these people did not want the clergy insulted and persecuted or their influence seriously diminished, but they did want them kept in their place, the place assigned to them in modern society by Napoleon.

Not less unpopular than the *Loi Falloux*, though much less important in its further consequences, was the Electoral Law of

May 31st, 1850. It maintained manhood suffrage in principle but in fact disfranchised about three million voters. Any person convicted of a political offence, however trivial, was deprived of the vote, and no one's name could be placed on the roll of electors unless he had lived for three years in the same district. The first requirement injured only the Jacobins and socialists, while the second immediately disfranchised very many of the urban poor, obliged as they were, in search of employment, to change their homes frequently. Manhood suffrage was one of the few principles common to all the republicans. Resistance to clerical encroachments, the vote for all adult males, the republican form of government: these three things were the least that would satisfy even the mildest republican. Two of them were already abandoned. There remained only the third, the republic itself. But the republic was served by a President whose ambition was to become an Emperor, and by an Assembly most of whose members were monarchists. When we consider how quickly the republicans were discredited, how few months elapsed between the triumph of February 1848 and the first victories of reaction, it is surprising that the second republic had so long a life.

Both the *Loi Falloux* and the Electoral Law did some harm to the conservatives. If they had only done that harm and yet brought other benefits, the conservatives might have had reason enough to congratulate themselves. But they did not do the good expected of them. The church and the Catholics were not grateful to the Assembly for the *Loi Falloux*. Louis Napoleon was, they thought, the ally most worth having. The church has seldom allowed gratitude to divert her from what she has always considered her duty no less than her interest: to increase her influence to whatever pitch the rulers of the state are willing to tolerate. The church sought the strongest ally she could find, not because she was naturally respectful of power, but because the strongest ally was likely to be the most useful. And Louis Napoleon certainly needed the church, having as much to gain as to give. The *Loi Falloux* put the church into an excellent humour, but this new fund of good will was lavished on the enemy of the Assembly that made the law. Louis Napoleon was also to make a little capital out of the Electoral Law; he opposed it and so once again appeared better disposed to democracy than did the deputies. But his gain in this case was probably much smaller. The republicans were already his enemies and were not deceived by his gesture, while the great mass of peasants, who neither committed political offences nor changed their homes, cared little who was deprived of his vote. Not that the peasant cared nothing for his own vote. He knew its value, though he may have estimated it in his own way. It was something he could use, should the need arise, to protest against the disturbers of order and property. It was also something given away free, and could always be sold, for a promise at least, if not for something more substantial. It was certainly worth having. But the peasant, except where he was beginning to listen to the republicans, did not think of the vote as an act of consent and a right to which every man is entitled. He was not displeased to see so many people deprived of it by the new Electoral Law.

Louis Napoleon had few of the gifts that make a man formidable to his fellow-men. He might have been born a king, so little did his personal qualities raise him above the general level of mankind. But he was shrewd, single-minded and willing to take risks. His silence gave him an advantage over more loquacious men; he came to know them better than they knew him and was able to profit by their mistakes. His knowledge of France and the French was not profound, but as an adventurer and a foreigner he was without prejudices. It is not a deep insight but coolness and common sense that enable a man to make his calculations accurately when he is playing for power. Louis Napoleon knew that he need not fear the conservatives too much. They were not popular, they were not united, and they were too explicit; they were without faith in a cause and yet full of prejudices and anxieties, too often loudly expressed; they were clever and quarrelsome. If they were at all to be feared, it was because most of the generals, especially in Paris, were Orleanists or Legitimists. But the troops, the non-commissioned and junior officers, were either Bonapartists or nothing. No pretender to the throne could be a hero to them except the nephew of the great Napoleon. The President knew that it was only a question of putting his friends into a few key positions and France might be his for the taking.

If there was a real danger, it came from the republicans. The reports that flowed into the Ministry of the Interior from every part of the country proved that they were making great progress. In the small towns they were making converts among the lower middle class, in the villages among the peasants. They were persuading them that they had nothing to fear from the workers, that social reform would leave their property and savings untouched. The peasants, except in the north and west, had no affection or respect for the well-to-do. If they were not democrats, they were certainly egalitarians. Now that property was no longer endangered, now that there was no bloodshed in Paris, they were not always unwilling to listen to the republicans. The republicans did not, like Louis Napoleon, appeal to their fears but to their self-respect, to their feelings as free and hard-working Frenchmen. Liberty, equality and fraternity were not empty words to a class of people who had gained so much by the first revolution. The republicans, while they were still strangers, creators of disorder in far-off cities, had seemed to the peasants the most dangerous of politicians; but now that their message was preached in the villages, often in the familiar voice of the local schoolmaster, it was found congenial. Justice was what the republicans spoke of, as if it were a thing everywhere protective and comfortable to the poor and dangerous only to the rich. This was a message the peasants could understand; it was, indeed, the first political message that ever came their way. If it was congenial to the minority of the peasants who heard it, it was exciting to the artisans and the poorer townsmen. The secret societies that now flourished in so many of the small towns in three-quarters of provincial France discussed only democracy and social reform; the word *socialism* was still too strong for them. But they did believe that theirs was the cause of the humble. They were united in their distrust of the rich and the powerful, the monarchists, the wealthy merchants and capitalists, and the church.

Reaction made slow progress in France. It began in June 1848 and did not triumph until December 1851. The manner of its progress was not edifying. Its sponsors had the power, or else they could not have succeeded. But their use of it discredited them; they were clumsy, vindictive, petty and ridiculous. Louis Napoleon was rather more skilful and even, perhaps, more dignified than the conservatives. When at last he seized power, the nation, except for its large republican minority, accepted the accomplished fact; but it accepted it with relief and not with enthusiasm. Napoleon seemed the best that providence had to offer France, and she made the best of him. But she never gave herself to him as she had done to his uncle or as Germany was to do to Hitler.

The republicans have often been blamed for their pacifism and blind confidence. They were preparing for the elections of 1852, which would give them, they hoped, a spectacular success. It never occurred to most of them that they might be forestalled, that the President might make a *coup d'état* before the elections were held.

The republicans were perhaps not as unwise as their critics say, or, if they were so, their lack of wisdom added little to the harm done to them. They expected a *coup d'état* after the elections and they collected what arms they could to resist it. Such a *coup d'état*, deliberately prepared to set aside the people's will, would, they thought, be recognised by everyone for what it was, an act of naked aggression. If the republicans used force, except to resist force, they would make enemies of the very classes whose confidence they were now gaining. They could not afford to forestall the President; they must wait for him to take the initiative. It seemed to them most probable that he would resort to force only when he found he could not manage the elections. They miscalculated, but their error was not unnatural. Louis Napoleon had pretended so long to be a democrat that they thought he would not throw off the mask until he had to. They had no precedents to guide them. When the first Bonaparte prepared the *coup* of the 18th Brumaire, circumstances had been quite different. Besides, the uncle, when he made his bid for power, was already the most famous soldier in Europe, while the nephew had never yet won a victory, except at the polls. Though by 1851, much more was known about him than his surname, he was still misunderstood and depreciated. The republicans knew they were making swift and quiet progress; they also knew they were so poorly armed that they could fight only on the defensive and in a popular cause. Their peaceful behaviour was winning them friends where they could never have expected them two or three years earlier; and most people believed them much weaker than they actually were. Their best policy, they thought, was to

H

remain as inconspicuous as they could, so that no one should be tempted to provoke them before the next elections. They could not know for certain when the expected blow would fall; they could prepare to meet it only when their influence with the people, at last made known to everyone, would oblige their enemy to strike or else abandon hope of absolute power. The republicans made many fewer mistakes between 1849 and 1851 than in 1848. They could hardly have parried the blow that was aimed at them in 1851. As it was, their aggressor, though he succeeded in his purpose, made bitter and irreconcilable enemies, enemies less unpopular and more respected than they had ever been before. The second republic, whose death was expected for three years before it died, was killed at last and as easily as the July Monarchy. It had lived a much shorter life. But when it died it was much more regretted. That, in spite of all their illusions and mistakes, was the achievement of the republicans in three and three-quarter years.

Louis Napoleon was in no hurry to seize absolute power. The republicans could do him no harm until the next elections, until 1852. That gave him two and a half years, should he need the time, to settle his account with the conservatives. He broke with them, as we have seen, in October 1849, when he dismissed the Odilon Barrot ministry; and then he waited over two years before he made his *coup d'état* in December 1851. He could afford to wait; and by waiting he had time to make himself popular with the troops, to come to terms with the church and to let the conservatives irritate each other and the people. The conservatives did try to settle the vexed question of the succession to the throne. It was suggested that the Legitimist pretender, the Comte de Chambord, who was childless, should be accepted by all the royalists. His successor according to law would then be the Comte de Paris, the Orleanist pretender. It was hoped this compromise might satisfy both the Legitimists and the Orleanists. It was the compromise they eventually accepted in 1873. But in 1850 it was less attractive to both parties than it became twenty-three years later. Many of the Legitimists said that the accession of Chambord would be a victory for the principle of the Divine Right of Kings; it would be a blessing for France and a defeat at the hands of God for all republicans, liberals and Bonapartists, that is to say, though Legitimists might pretend to believe otherwise, for the great majority of Frenchmen. The Orleanists disliked these constant references to God and right divine. They wanted a manageable king, a symbol of property and order, a man on good terms with the church but no nearer to God than his political advisers, a quiet, ordinary, accessible king who believed in peace and prosperity. Apart from this matter of principle, there were also personal ambitions. The Comte de Chambord was an ageing man in 1873; in 1850 he was only thirty years old and might expect a long life. The Duchess of Orleans, the mother of the Comte de Paris, was not willing that her son's reign should be postponed indefinitely. She was encouraged to be firm by Thiers, who knew he could expect nothing from a Legitimist king. The part he had played in 1830 was, he thought, more than Chambord could forgive. At the end of 1850 the royalists were still quarrelling; and their quarrels had discouraged them and sapped their energy.

V. THE LAST MONTHS OF THE REPUBLIC

The conservatives felt safe until January 1851. Until that time General Changarnier, an Orleanist, remained in command of the National Guard and the regular troops in Paris. Changarnier was talkative and conceited. He explained that, according to the constitution, though the President was the Commander-in-Chief, only the Assembly had the right to set the armed forces in motion. A formal order from the President of the Assembly would, he said, be enough to enable him to arrest the President of the Republic and send him to the Fort of Vincennes. But Changarnier forgot that the strength of the Assembly lay in his power, and the power of men like him, to resist Louis Napoleon's orders. The President was making what military appointments he liked, winning the loyalty of ambitious officers serving in Africa and transferring them to metropolitan commands. No one could contest his right to do so, and yet the officers he promoted were just as sure of the obedience of their troops as their royalist predecessors. Indeed, they were more sure, for the troops still preferred any sort of a Bonaparte to Bourbon kings and middle-class parliaments. When Louis Napoleon felt strong enough to act, he quietly dismissed Changarnier. The conservatives found they could not retaliate. They made do with a mere vote of no confidence in the government, but the motion that embodied it did not even mention Changarnier's dismissal. Thiers tried to persuade the Assembly to take a braver stand. If they were satisfied with so tame a motion, he said, everyone would know they had surrendered to the President.

It was then that Thiers told the Assembly that, if they yielded on this issue, the Empire, though it might not be called by that name, was re-established. But the Assembly would not take his advice. They felt there was nothing to be done except to save appearances. Thiers had only made their weakness more obvious. Changarnier's dismissal excited the politicians but left the people indifferent. It was merely the most important of the many moves that the President felt he must make if he were to destroy the republic quickly and without danger of civil war. He needed just ten months more to complete his arrangements. He had to put his supporters where he wanted them and he had to see to it that the troops were persuaded that no civil court would ever hold them responsible for carrying out whatever orders their superior officers might give them. It takes time to allay the fears and ease the consciences of many thousands of men. Besides, Louis Napoleon had also to buy support in the Assembly, if only to ensure that nothing was done to weaken his position at law. He was not the leader of an army of fanatics, on whose organised devotion he could count in all circumstances. It was good politics, therefore, to put as small a burden as possible on his supporters' consciences.

Just before the *coup d'état*, Louis Napoleon made a move to divide his opponents. He invited the Assembly to repeal the Electoral Law of 1849. The conservatives of course refused, and the republicans were incensed against them. Louis Napoleon wanted to prevent a last-minute coalition of the conservatives and republicans in the Assembly, a coalition to prevent his expected *coup d'état*. He made the republicans so angry with the conservatives that they later voted against a motion to allow the President of the Assembly, should he think it necessary, to require the obedience of the army. This proposal, had it been passed, would certainly have unsettled many a soldierly conscience, and it might just possibly have prevented the *coup d'état*. From this last danger the President was saved, not only by the republicans, but by a number of deputies he had won over to his side. These deputies were disgusted with the never-ending quarrels and intrigues in the Assembly; they felt sure the President would win in the end and they decided to support him, and so earn their share of the rewards of inevitable victory. Who can say that they loved themselves better than their country? The various friends of liberty were each other's enemies; and liberty could not survive their quarrels. Might it not be wisdom to prefer the dictatorship of a mild, patient and civilian Bonaparte to the trickery, the bitterness, the unceasing and always-changing disputes of frantic and ambitious parliamentarians?

The republicans did not, by voting against the proposal, make as big a mistake as their critics have said. They had no more reason to trust the conservatives than to trust the President; they had to choose the lesser of two evils. They knew that Louis Napoleon wanted absolute power, but this was all they knew against him. On the other hand, the conservatives were the very men who had ruled France from 1815 to 1848, who had always persecuted the republicans and been indifferent to the poor. Why then should they help to place armed power in the hands of a conservative Assembly? The republicans may in fact have chosen the greater of two evils, or, rather, have taken the greater of two risks. This was the balance of advantages facing them as it now appears to most French historians. We may well agree with the historians and yet see that it was difficult for anyone placed in the position of the republicans in 1851 to strike a true account. The republicans were certainly apt to be blinded by their faith. They, just as much as anyone, expected a *coup d'état*, and yet they found it more difficult than other people to believe it could succeed. The French, they thought, were not in 1851 what they had been in 1799. If Louis Napoleon attempted a *coup d'état*, they would resist him. "There is no danger," said one of the republicans, "and if there were a danger, there is always an invisible sentinel that guards us; that sentinel is the people." The republicans were always optimists. This confidence in the future was their weakness as well as their strength.

The *coup d'état*, so long expected, when at last it came, took everyone by surprise. The common opinion is that it was accepted with relief by a people tired of the politicians and their intrigues. The ease with which Louis Napoleon delivered his blow and the immense majorities that voted for him at subsequent plebiscites are alleged in evidence of his popularity. The new dictator and his friends offered the world an explanation of their success that was certainly plausible. Their account, the official myth of the Second Empire, is that the *coup d'état* was accepted with enthusiasm and relief by a people equally tired of royalists and republicans and living in daily fear of a new revolution. The Prince-President, so soon to become Emperor, was the saviour of his people; if he had destroyed liberty it was only for their sake. Who could pretend that the royalists, whether Legitimists or Orleanists, really cared for liberty? And the republicans, who talked about liberty so much, had they not tried, though only a minority, to terrorise and dominate France? The conservatives and republicans were in this respect alike: they were ambitious and unscrupulous minorities who would stick at nothing to gain power. The only difference between them was that the republicans exploited the grievances of the poor and the conservatives the prejudices of the rich, that the republicans preferred violence and the conservatives intrigue. The President alone could speak for the nation, reassure the peasants and maintain order. He was not the tool of the privileged and yet he was the champion of property; he was also the friend of all the great institutions on which the moral health and security of the nation depended; he was on good terms with the church and on excellent terms with the army.

This, and variations on it, made up the official myth, believed by most people, even by many who would have liked to think otherwise, so neatly did the explanation seem to fit the visible facts. Fortunately for the historian, it is always the interest of the absolute ruler that some people in his country should tell the truth. The police must watch what happens and, if they are to be of use to their master, must send him accurate accounts of what they see. These accounts, the police reports of 1851, have been studied. It is from them, indeed, that historians have learnt two things that quite destroy the official myth; they have learnt that France was seldom quieter than in 1851, and that there was widespread resistance to the *coup d'état*. France in December 1851 neither needed nor wanted to be saved from anyone, except from her saviour.

The resistance was not fierce but it was widespread. It also happened where it was least expected. It failed of its effect and passed unnoticed, except by the police, just because its character was so unexpected. The republicans in the small towns and the villages took to arms, but they could not combine their efforts and achieve any spectacular success unless Paris and the larger towns gave them the lead. Now, it was precisely in the capital and the great towns that the authorities expected violent resistance; and they therefore took every precaution against it. When the republicans in the country towns and villages heard that their friends in Lyon, Marseilles, Bordeaux and Toulouse, not to speak of Paris, had either not moved at all or had given up the fight almost as soon as they began it, they dispersed and went home. It was above all the failure of Paris to resist effectively that discouraged the republicans everywhere. All eyes were on the capital, in 1851 as in 1848 and 1830, and this time there were far more people willing to follow where Paris led. That there could be a fight for liberty not led by Paris occurred to no one. But Paris was held in a tighter grip than any other part of France.

It is not true that the Parisians did nothing to resist Louis Napoleon's *coup*. The republican deputies established a committee to organise a revolt in the capital. The workers were not indifferent to the appeals made to them. They built barricades, but this time they were defeated before they could consolidate their positions. There was, in fact, considerable resistance in Paris, where nearly 160 persons, most of them working men, were killed in the fighting. No doubt, the Paris workers were less willing to risk their lives than they had sometimes been in the past; they had suffered a great letting of blood in June 1848 and had not yet recovered from its effects. Paris was weaker than she had been and more closely watched; she was not able to stand up against Louis Napoleon's aggression as strongly as the republicans hoped. But she was not indifferent. Paris was more republican than she had ever been. She was never reconciled with the aggressor of December 2nd. Lyon, Marseilles, Bordeaux and Toulouse were also full of police and troops; the republicans there could do nothing but lie low. Their inaction paralysed the Jacobins in the districts where they had made the greatest progress during the last three years.

What resistance there was was certainly short-lived. In many places it died out before it could be put down. But there was so much of it scattered here and there over the whole country that a state of siege was proclaimed in thirty-two departments. There were armed revolts in several small towns in the south-west, and at Vic-Fezensac 1,500 peasants assembled to march on Auch, the capital of the department of the Gers. Most of these revolts happened in places where there had been almost no republicans in 1848.

There is no evidence, indeed, that any large class of people welcomed the *coup d'état*. Most of the peasants, still suspicious of the republicans, accepted it as they accepted anything done by the government, provided that they stood to lose nothing by it. The conservatives resented the aggression but moved not a finger to resist it. Only the army thought the new state of France better than the old one. Even the clergy were at first reserved; they could not regret the change and might well hope to profit by it. But before they would give their whole-hearted support, Louis Napoleon had to go out of his way to please them. The church was not a party to the *coup d'état*. The plot was hatched by the future Emperor and his personal friends. As a former Carbonaro, he was in his element. His earlier plots, which had led to his imprisonment at Ham, had failed because the police and the army were against him. This time both these precious allies supported him. And as soon as his plot succeeded, he hastened to assure the bishops of his good will. Within a few days of its happening the *coup d'état* received the blessing of the church. Even Montalembert and the Catholic Liberals approved it for a time; and if they quickly turned against the new dictator it was only because he confiscated the property of the House of Orleans.

Chapter Five

THE SECOND EMPIRE

I. THE YEARS OF REPRESSION

THE repression after the *coup d'état* was worse than anything done by a French government since the Terror. Over twenty-six thousand persons, nearly all of them republicans, were arrested and brought to trial before special commissions. This form of trial was condemned as an outrage to justice, a procedure unworthy of a civilised government. None of the Bourbon kings since 1815 had done anything so shocking to respectable opinion. The President's excuse was that there were too many people arrested to enable them all to be tried by the ordinary courts. On December 8th a decree was published allowing the transportation to Guiana or North Africa of any person convicted of belonging to a secret society or of trying to move out of a district where a state of siege was proclaimed. This decree appeared terrible to a people accustomed to the milder standards of the last century. It is true that working men were shot down by the thousand in the streets of Paris in June 1848 and then again in May 1871, but they were rebels who had defied the only authority that could be called legitimate by the democratic standards they themselves professed. The repression that followed the *coup d'état* was something quite different; it was aimed at men who had taken up arms or who were suspected of having intended to take up arms against a political aggressor, against a President who had broken his oath to the constitution. If Louis Napoleon's action was approved, as he said it was, by the great majority of the people, if they overlooked its illegality only because they were convinced it was necessary, why was the President so brutally repressive? His special commissions did their work so thoroughly that their purpose was soon evident; they were not only punishing the guilty but were putting out of the way every locally influential republican who might be a nuisance to the President. Their business was not to dispense justice but to make a political purge. As only the authorities knew how strong the republicans really were and the President was anxious to persuade everyone that they were an insignificant minority, these precautions seemed excessive. The French are a sensible, humane and frugal people; they were not impressed by a large repression to put down an insignificant and yet somehow very dangerous set of people.

In 1852 it was generally believed, except by the Ministry of the Interior and the police, that republicanism was practically destroyed. The republicans themselves were not aware how widespread their disconnected efforts at resistance had been. They were discouraged by their easy defeat. Every separate group of insurgents or would-be insurgents had felt isolated from the rest; every group had felt that their own failure was due to the pusillanimity of the others. After the buoyant optimism of the last months before December 2nd, there succeeded a mood of frustration and despair. The republicans thought everything was lost. They did not know how formidable they had seemed to the only people able to watch their activities.

It was still too early for the republicans to count the assets they had acquired since 1848. For four years France had been a republic, and for the first of those years the republicans had governed her. It had taken the forces of reaction three years to destroy the republic. Such memories meant nothing to the republicans in 1852; their defeat was too recent and too humiliating. But as the years passed, they became a comfort and an inspiration. What had once been done might be done again. And meanwhile France was becoming more industrial, more urban and more literate. She was becoming the sort of country that might be willing to listen seriously to the republicans.

The very fact that the republicans in the large towns had been unable to move was in one way an advantage to them; they had exposed themselves less than their comrades in smaller places. Fewer of them were arrested and many of their secret societies survived the repression. Party discipline was not entirely destroyed. When the first mood of despair was over, exasperation at their too easy defeat served to keep them active. Thus it was that, though resistance to the *coup d'état* had mostly happened in the smaller towns and villages, it was the large towns, and Paris especially, that were Napoleon's most irreconcilable and dangerous enemies while he was Emperor.

I do not wish to suggest that Napoleon III was not popular. He was as popular as anyone who ruled France since Waterloo. The peasants liked him; so, too, did the army and the church. The rich, when they saw how much he was prepared to do for industry and commerce, also learnt to think better of him. He was liked, tolerated, approved of or found useful by many millions of Frenchmen; but only a few were devoted to him either as a person or a ruler. On the other hand, he was more bitterly hated, and by many more people, than either Charles X or Louis Philippe. He was at once the most liked and the most hated ruler of modern France. And hatred is a stronger emotion than liking, toleration or approval.

At the plebiscite of December 31st, 1851, the French were invited to vote that they "desired the maintenance of the authority of Louis Napoleon Bonaparte and granted to him the powers necessary to establish a constitution . . ." When the votes were counted, it was found that seven and a half millions were cast in favour of the President and less than 650,000 against him. The government at first wanted open voting but decided at last that the ballot should be secret. This decision pleased the liberals all over Europe who were watching events in France. It seemed to them a guarantee that the voting would be free. But Napoleon and his advisers had another motive. They had made the *coup d'état* to forestall the free elections of 1852. It is therefore not unfair to them to suppose they were not very interested in the accurate representation of the people's will. What they wanted was to let fear operate untrammelled by shame. Every man knew how the authorities expected him to vote, and most men were anxious, either because they approved, or were afraid, or thought it prudent, to do what was expected of them. Many people believed that, though the ballot might be called secret, the authorities would in any case know how they had voted. The secrecy of the ballot would not, if they voted against the President, protect them from his police, but it might spare them the reproaches and abuse of their friends. The ballot was therefore made secret so that the timid might indulge their weakness without fear of the bold. The republicans were at that time the victims of a police repression of exceptional severity; only the bravest of them had not lost their nerve. The secret ballot would ensure that the brave kept their courage to themselves. Not that Louis Napoleon feared a majority against him. If the plebiscite had been as free as it could have been made, he would still have triumphed. But a majority was not enough for him. He also wanted to prove that only an insignificant minority were against him. Terror combined with the secret ballot, the means so often used since his time by other dictators, first proved effective on December 31st, 1851.

The new constitution, published on January 24th, 1852, was an imitation of the one set up after the 18th Brumaire by the first Bonaparte. The President, elected for ten years, initiated all legislation and could veto it. He could also, on his sole authority, declare a state of siege in any part of France. The lower chamber, the *Corps Législatif*, was to be elected for six years by manhood suffrage. It could discuss and vote only on the bills put before it by the government, whose sole responsibility was to the President. The *Corps Législatif* could not even discuss an amendment to a bill without first getting permission from the Council of State, a body of officials appointed by the President; nor could it interpellate the government or vote an address in reply to a message from the President. The Senate, made up of senators ex officio and of persons nominated by the President, was not a legislative chamber. Its business was to consider the laws passed by the *Corps Législatif* and to annul them if they were unconstitutional. It could also publish decrees interpreting the constitution. When the President a year later assumed the imperial title, there was no need to make any important change in the constitution. It had already concentrated all real power in the hands of one man.

Louis Napoleon and his friends established a régime more hostile to liberty than France had known since 1814. The press was muzzled and every political and even professional association that might be dangerous to the government suppressed. Of two hundred and twenty-one co-operative and friendly societies, only fifteen were allowed to survive. The National Guard, beloved of

all French governments whose power depended on a narrow
franchise and exclusive middle-class support, was abolished.
Napoleon relied entirely upon the army and the police. Workers'
passports, the *livrets* imposed upon them by Napoleon I, were
reintroduced. Napoleon III established a more severe and
efficient police administration than either Louis XVIII, Charles
X or Louis Philippe had done. France had often known repressive
government, abuse of power and discrimination against the poor.
But she was an efficient police state only twice in her history:
from 1800 to 1814, and from 1852 to 1860. In 1860 Louis
Napoleon decided to give France her head a little, and he gradually loosed his hold on her, until the Empire became liberal. The
strength of the opposition so quickly revealed, the savagery of
the attacks made on him in his last years, prove how much he was
hated. France felt humiliated by him long before Sedan: not all
France, perhaps, but a large and important minority of Frenchmen, who had been taught by the republicans that it was shameful
for men not to be free.

During the first part of his reign, Napoleon's great ally—the
army and the police were his instruments rather than his allies—
was the church. Napoleon III was more popular, bolder, and a
better politician than Louis Philippe or Charles X. He was, in the
opinion of the church, an ally better worth having. There was
certainly some little warmth in the support given by the clergy to
the new Emperor. The church, of course, always put her own
interests first; the French clergy had long distinguished the
France they loved from the impermanent régimes imposed on her.
The church, as she was eventually to prove, was quite ready,
should the necessity arise, to abandon Napoleon III. But until
1859 she did believe that France had at last the ruler the church
needed. She accepted Napoleon with relief and confidence and
was grateful to God for having sent him. The Emperor wanted
to be both popular and absolute. What ambition could the
church better understand and sympathise with? Was it not, after
all, her own ambition?

The support of Napoleon by the church weakened the royalists.
The Legitimists and Orleanists were both upper-class parties,
except in the few parts of France where the peasants, artisans and
small shopkeepers shared the beliefs of the nobles and the wealthy.

Otherwise, what support they had ever had from the poor, they had always owed to the clergy, at those times when the church had been the ally of Charles X and Louis Philippe. It was also to the clergy that the conservatives of 1849 had owed their electoral triumph. Now that the priests no longer supported them, the Legitimists and Orleanists were both greatly diminished. The Legitimists were now no more than the party of the old nobility, and the Orleanists the party of the upper middle class. In the Legislative Assembly of 1849 the Orleanists had outnumbered the Legitimists; they could usually count on wider support. But they were also more easily won from their allegiance. They did not, like the Legitimists, believe that their candidate for the throne was king by divine right. If Napoleon III dealt justly with the world of business, why should he not rule France in the place of the Count of Paris? Not all the Orleanists argued like this; many of them wanted power, either in Paris or locally, and they resented Napoleon's monopoly of it. The Legitimists, on the other hand, could not decently accommodate their principles to the times. Whether they were politically ambitious or not, however well Napoleon might govern, there was, by their principles, only one man in the world to whom the throne rightfully belonged. While that man was kept out of his inheritance, there could be no justice in France.

Their electoral victories in 1849 and 1871, when there was manhood suffrage and voting was free, has made many people believe that the royalists were stronger than they really were. Both these elections were held in unusual circumstances, and the people, when voting for the royalists, had other things than royalty in mind. The same electorate that returned the conservative majority of 1849 had, only a few months earlier, voted, in even greater numbers, for Louis Bonaparte as President of France. No one, not even the Orleanists who hoped to manage him, believed that either Louis Bonaparte or those who voted for him intended to prepare the way for either sort of Bourbon restoration. And in 1871, those who voted for the conservatives voted for peace. They would not vote republican because the republic wanted to continue the war. As Napoleon III was a prisoner and Bonapartism in disgrace, there was nothing they could do except vote for royalist candidates. There is no evi-

dence that France was ever strongly royalist at any time since
the eighteenth century.

Napoleon had the big voting battalions; he had also the
alliance of the church, the devotion of the army and the loyalty of
the officials. This last is a loyalty that belongs by right of conquest to whomsoever captures the state without trying (or being
accused of doing so) to "overturn" society.[1] The peasants, the
army and the officials never deserted Napoleon until the Prussians
defeated him; he was as much to their taste as any alternative
they could think of. He had never needed to get rid of any but
the highest officials and general officers; most of the other
professional servants of the state, civil and military, not very well
paid, jealous of their superiors, fond of power and obedience,
were as naturally attracted to Napoleon as their German equi-
valents in the 1930s to Adolf Hitler.

To give guidance to those who felt the need for it, Napoleon
introduced the official candidature at general elections. Hitherto,
all candidates had had the same status. Government candidates
had been given whatever help the police and the prefects could
give them, but all this had been done unofficially. Every candidate had been put up by his party or personal supporters;
whether he approved of the government or not, the prefect and
other public officials were not supposed to intervene openly
either for or against him. The official candidature was therefore
an innovation. Most of the peasants did not mind it; they were
quite pleased to be told how to vote. They liked manhood
suffrage, they liked to think they were not ignored. Orderly
government was, they thought, an excellent thing, and it was
their duty and interest to support it. Otherwise, except where the
republicans had converted them, they did not want to bother their
heads about politics. Government had never been their business,
but unfortunately governments sometimes interfered with them
in unexpected ways or else troubles they could not ignore happened in Paris and the other large towns. But Napoleon never
interfered with them, he maintained good order and flattered
them, and in return they gave him their votes.

---

[1] The great majority of the republicans had, of course, no intention of "over-
turning" society. But their enemies imputed this motive to them, and the officials,
especially the police, believed them.

What of the republican and socialist movements during the Second Empire? The republicans and socialists had lost their leaders. Blanqui, Raspail, Albert and Huber were all in prison. They had been the first victims of reaction, going to prison in 1848 and kept there longer than anyone else. Barbès, imprisoned with the others, was later released at the prayer of George Sand and went into voluntary exile in Holland. The affair of June 13th, 1849, had led to the imprisonment of several of the Jacobin leaders and to the flight abroad of Ledru-Rollin and Louis Blanc. The republican propaganda of 1849–51 and the resistance to the *coup d'état* had been directed by a new generation of local leaders, none of them famous throughout France. Their quiet propaganda, their short resistance and their local reputations had deceived everyone, except the authorities, about their importance. These local leaders had, many of them, fled the country after the *coup d'état* or had fallen victims to the proscription that followed it. The ones who had neither fled nor had been arrested lay low. The republicans and socialists were leaderless and therefore quiescent. The first years of the Second Empire, like the middle years of the July Monarchy, were years of silence for the Jacobins and revolutionaries left in France.

But the exiles were not silent. The most important of them, Ledru-Rollin and Louis Blanc, men with European reputations, were in London. So, too, were Félix Pyat and Delescluze, younger men who were to carry on the Jacobin tradition during the Second Empire and the Commune. Félix Pyat formed a society in London called *La Commune Révolutionnaire* in opposition to the society *La Révolution* dominated by Ledru-Rollin, whom Pyat thought tame and ineffective. Both the Rollinists and the Pyatists, as they were called, kept away from socialists like Louis Blanc and Pierre Leroux. The radical exiles in London saw a good deal of Mazzini, and it was he who persuaded them that the revolution of 1848 had failed because the republicans had been too closely associated with the socialists. Mazzini himself would have nothing to do with Louis Blanc, whom he thought responsible for the failure of the revolution. If Louis Blanc had not encouraged the workers, if he had not forced the establishment of the Luxembourg Commission and the National Workshops, the middle class and the peasants would never have been frightened of the revolution. Mazzini, Ledru-Rollin and Kossuth, the three most famous of the London exiles, republicans but not socialists, thought themselves a sort of triumvirate whose duty was to guide the democratic movement all over the Continent. Ledru-Rollin and Mazzini formed in 1851 the *European Democratic Committee*, interested in political questions only and leaving socialist doctrines severely alone. The London exiles were in some respects better off than the others. England was too powerful a country to want to please Louis Napoleon by pestering his enemies. But the climate, the language and the polite indifference of their English hosts discouraged the exiles. They had once been powerful and they had since lost their power without quite knowing how it was they had lost it; they still believed that without them the republicans in France could do nothing. They felt indispensable and were yet daily reminded of their insignificance. They were sharply critical of everything that had happened in France since their departure. A few of the exiles on British territory found some relief from frustration and anxiety in literature. Victor Hugo wrote his *Châtiments*, *Napoleon le Petit*, and also other works not concerned with politics. Louis Blanc wrote a *History of the Revolution of 1848*. These books, and others written by the exiles, as well as pamphlets and newspapers, were smuggled into France. They formed a considerable part of the secret literature that kept up the courage of the republicans during their darkest years.

The republicans who fled after the *coup d'état* mostly went to Belgium and Switzerland. They were not famous, they had never had power to lose; they were more modest and more adaptable than the exiles of 1849. They were well enough liked in Belgium, by the people if not by the police. They taught, lectured and made speeches; and their presence added vigour and variety to Belgian intellectual life. But the authorities, anxious not to offend Louis Napoleon, watched their movements and made difficulties for them. After a time, many of them moved to Switzerland or England. It was in French Switzerland that the exiles felt most at home and could most easily earn their livings.

The exiles kept closely in touch with the republicans in France. The importance of these contacts is proved by the greater activity of the republicans in the districts nearest the frontiers.

I

The republicans had made most of their converts, in the two years before the *coup d'état*, in four areas: in the industrial districts of the north-east, in Alsace-Lorraine, in the Rhône valley and in the south-west. The constant coming and going across the Belgian and Swiss frontiers kept republicanism alive in three of these areas, but in the fourth, the south-west, furthest removed from these frontiers, the republicans, so recently more active than anywhere else, sank for a time into apathy.

The exiles did not appear negligible to Napoleon. He did not like having enemies and he wanted all the security he could get. He tried, if not to win over, then at least to come to some sort of terms with the exiles. The year after the *coup d'état*, they were invited to return to France provided only that they promised to refrain from all political activity. Most of them refused this conditional amnesty. In March 1856 Louis Napoleon made another attempt at reconciliation. The *Moniteur* published an invitation to every exile to return provided he recognised the existing government. This condition, much easier than the first in 1852, made the amnesty more attractive, and a considerable number of exiles returned to France. But none of the leaders would accept anything less than an unconditional amnesty. It was not till 1859 that the Emperor, on indifferent terms with the church and looking for support elsewhere, at last decided to allow any exile (except Ledru-Rollin, whom the authorities chose to consider an ordinary criminal) to return without requiring any promise of him. Louis Blanc and a few others would not accept the amnesty, saying it was absurd for a criminal to pardon his victims. But the great majority of the exiles had had enough of life abroad and they flocked back to France. The granting of this unconditional amnesty brought to an end the first and the blackest period of Napoleon's reign. It was not merely a concession; it was also, in a way, a confession of weakness. The great majority of Frenchmen were as docile as ever, and yet the all-powerful ruler of France felt the need to placate a hostile minority. So little did the prince who had plotted and tricked his way to the throne put his trust in majorities.

From 1851 to 1859 the republicans in France were quiescent but not altogether inactive. While the conflict between radicalism and reaction lasted, from the end of 1848 till the *coup d'état*, the moderate republicans had been reduced to insignificance. Those who believed the republic worth fighting for moved to the left, while the others joined the conservatives. But when that conflict ended with the complete victory of reaction, the voice of the moderate republicans, no longer drowned by the noise of lustier combatants, was heard once more. They alone had survived the proscription and need not be silent for fear of punishment. They had always been respectable. Everyone had voted for them nearly four years ago. If they had been disregarded in the interval, it was only because most men not indifferent to politics had felt the need to take sides in a conflict to which the moderates could hardly be an effective party. Their insignificance during the last three years now stood the moderate republicans in good stead. They had survived because no one had feared them. They now had no rivals who were also opponents of the Emperor, and the Emperor was prepared to tolerate them.

The leaders of the moderate republicans (Cavaignac, Goudchaux, Grévy, Favre, Simon, etc.) lived in Paris. There they carried on the cautious but effective propaganda that was their special gift. They held salons, they had a great influence in the Latin quarter and they published newspapers. They kept republicanism alive in the circles in which it had already been vigorous during the July Monarchy; and when it was again possible to offer parliamentary opposition to the new régime, it was they who offered it. Their services to the republican cause must be recognised. They were the same from 1851 to 1870 as they had been from 1830 to 1848. They made republicanism respectable; they kept it alive among the intellectuals and the social class from which the civil servants, judges and officers were also drawn. The moderate republicans in Napoleon III's time did another service to their cause greater than any they had done before: they provided the third republic with its first generation of republican leaders, men like Gambetta, Ferry and Clémenceau. Soon after the revolution of 1848, the moderate republicans lost all power; but after 1870, in spite of the election of a royalist Assembly and the Paris Commune, they did not allow themselves to be thrust aside. They stood their ground and at last created the respectable bourgeois republic they had failed to create in 1848.

Of the moderate republican salons the most important were

those of Mme. d'Agoult and Jules Simon. It was in them that loyalty to the republic was kept alive among the cultured upper middle class. In the Latin Quarter there arose a new generation of republicans, students whose teachers were university professors who had lost their posts because of their refusal to take the oath of loyalty to the Emperor. These professors found work in a few private schools and colleges, controlled neither by the state nor the church. The most famous of them, the Collège Ste. Barbe, employed Jules Simon and Michelet. During their holidays, these republican teachers went abroad and met the exiles. It was they who brought up the next generation of republicans among the Paris students. The students had also their own salons, like that of Mme. Hérold, frequented by Picard and Émile Ollivier. It was there that Jules Ferry, after 1856, held his *conférences* at which the students met leading republicans. The studio of the painter Delestre, frequented by Clémenceau, was another favourite meeting place for young republicans.

Apart from the salons and the teachers, there were also two other instruments of republican propaganda, two newspapers, *Le Siècle*, edited by Havin, and *La Presse*, edited by Émile de Giradin and then by Nefftzer. Both had a large circulation for those days; indeed, *Le Siècle*, with a circulation of 36,500 in 1859, became at last the most popular newspaper in Paris. Nothing could be more moderate than the opposition of these two newspapers; yet it was important because it existed, because it was the only open criticism of the régime tolerated in Paris.

The moderate republicans, important in literary and academic circles, had almost no contact with the workers and peasants. It was only in Paris, where the traditional alliance of students and workers still survived, that they could have even an indirect influence outside these narrow circles. The workers had no reason to love the moderate republicans. On the other hand, if they wanted to express their hostility to Louis Napoleon, they could only do so by voting for moderate republican candidates at elections. At the first elections after the *coup d'état*, only three republicans had been elected, but they had refused to take their seats in a servile legislature. At the elections of 1857, seven republicans were elected, five in Paris and two in the provinces. The republicans in Paris, all of them moderates, polled almost as many votes as the official candidates. If the workers had not voted for them in considerable numbers, five would never have been elected. In the conditions then prevalent, with the police and other civil powers working against them, the elections in Paris in 1857 were a considerable moral victory for the moderate republicans.

Only the moderate republicans were tolerated by the police, so that their activities were alone visible. The Jacobins and the socialists worked in secret and no one can know just how active they were. The only records, more or less reliable, are the police reports; but it may well be that the police, at different times and places and for diverse reasons, either saw much less than was happening or else guessed at more than was there to be seen. What we can know for certain is that, not only in the large towns, but in all the districts won over to republicanism before the *coup d'état*, secret societies flourished. Those we know most about, because there were police spies in them, were the least formidable. The most effective were perhaps the smallest, the *chambrées* in the south of France, of which there appears to have been a great number. They mostly consisted of persons united by their hatred of the régime and by ties of friendship, who could therefore trust one another. Because they were small, devoted and self-reliant, the police found it difficult to keep track of them and almost impossible to introduce spies into them. It was the larger secret societies that suffered most. In Lyon there were so many secret societies of workmen that the police grew anxious in 1853 and decided, through their spies, to promote their amalgamation. The police also succeeded in getting one of their agents appointed secretary of the amalgamated society. From that moment everything undertaken by the Lyon workers was bound to fail, and they were exposed for the next seventeen years to just as much punishment as the police thought good for them. Napoleon III's police disliked the workers more than any other section of the people.

There were plots and attempted assassinations, not only by Italian enemies of the ex-carbonari now become Emperor, but by French students and workmen. There were four real plots during the first two years of the reign, quite apart from several others possibly invented by the police. The Italians, indeed, gave

Louis Napoleon two years' grace before plotting his assassination. But his French enemies were active from the beginning, and nothing he could do, could, in their eyes, restore his right to be alive. For an important minority of Frenchmen, Napoleon was a political criminal, a man of blood. When in January 1858 Orsini made his attempt on the Emperor's life, there were many people in Paris who sympathised with the would-be assassin. The advocate who defended Orsini at his trial, Jules Favre, was so much admired for his spirited defence that he was elected to the *Corps Législatif* at a by-election in Paris in April 1858. Napoleon was bitterly hated; his power, the way it was got and the way it was used, was felt as a humiliation for France. The men who felt this hatred were only a minority, but they were a minority recruited from every class.

A few salons and newspapers, a few plots, and secret societies whose number was unknown to anyone—these were the only signs that republicanism and socialism were not yet dead. Most people saw nothing of any of them and heard of them only because the authorities took punitive action against them. That some republicanism survived the *coup d'état* was obvious; men would have believed it even without the reminders of the police. But socialism was, they thought, almost certainly dead. Nobody but a few cranks ever spoke of it. The workers had never understood it. They had fought for it without knowing what they were doing and had suffered for their folly. Socialism, so men thought, had been killed during the June days, and since then could hardly have come to life again. It was no longer discussed as a possible danger to society. It was, so men thought, a threat that France had survived. That such doctrines have a natural attraction for the working class, that they cannot be eradicated though their expression is forbidden—these were ideas not to be found in the philosophies of bourgeois and peasant. Only the authorities knew better. Seignobos in the sixth volume of Lavisse's *Histoire de la France Contemporaine* quotes a passage from the report of the *procureur général* of Lyon: "In talking to an artisan, you are almost certain to get to the point where he expounds a philosophical theory on the organisation of society. You will come across a certain elevation of language, but above all the deep conviction that a socialist system must at last prevail." What was true of

Lyon was certainly not less true of Paris. The workers had fought and suffered for socialism. Whether or not they understood what they were fighting for, it was a cause they would not abandon.

The reports of other officials prove that Jacobinism was still alive even in the south-west, the area furthest removed from the Belgian and Swiss frontiers and the English Channel. Some of the proscribed, after making a due submission, were pardoned only a year after the proscription. When they returned to their homes, they were received as martyrs, in the words of one report, "without noise but with an ill-disguised joy." They were respected locally and as much listened to as ever. They spoke more discreetly, but their influence was a cause of deep and often-repeated anxiety to the mayors and police officials.

II. THE REPUBLICAN REVIVAL

The years of quiescence and subterranean activity lasted until 1857. The elections of that year mark the beginning of the republican revival, or, rather, of the return of the republicans into the public life of France. They had always since 1849 been stronger than they knew. From 1857 onward they grew not only stronger but more conscious of their strength. At the elections seven republicans were returned, five in Paris and two in the provinces. Soon after one of them went over to the government and three others resigned their seats. Subsequent by-elections brought in two more, so that the eventual republican strength in the legislature was five. These five, Favre, Ollivier, Picard, Darimon and Hémon, were for six years the accredited spokesmen of the republicans in France. Their importance was much more than proportionate to their number, for it was well known that republicanism was very greatly under-represented in the legislature, that the five spoke for many more Frenchmen than were to be found in their constituencies. Besides, of all the deputies, they alone were not obsequious to power; and in a country like France, where courage and independence are always respected, this is an important moral asset. The five republicans were disliked, suspected and abused, but they were also listened to by men who knew that what they said counted for much more than their votes.

Until 1857 the republicans and socialists had done little more than keep up each other's courage and make converts among people they knew and could trust. From 1857 to 1863, they once again took the initiative. They took it not so much in the political as in the intellectual sphere. They began once more to publish books and to influence people they knew nothing of. In 1858 Proudhon published his greatest work, *De la Justice dans la Révolution et dans l'Église*. In it he taught that justice and religion are irreconcilable, that the love of justice is the mother of every virtue, that what he called human dignity is the best of all things, and that the readiness to defend it, always and with energy and if need be to one's own hurt, is in fact justice. This notion of justice implies social equality and therefore the transformation of the existing order; but what Proudhon prized most and most warmly praised was the dignity of the individual and his right to freedom, political, intellectual, economic and moral. This ideal of justice was, he thought, what had inspired the revolutionaries of France and the philosophers of Germany at their best. Proudhon still disapproved of the Jacobinism of the nineteenth century, the demagogic behaviour that was (he thought) a mere imitation of the Jacobins of 1793. This side of his teaching and his dislike of intervention on behalf of foreign liberals irritated many republicans. There was always something harsh and critical about his writings; there was a sharp edge to all his enthusiasms. But his influence was now at its greatest. The religiosity, the easy optimism, the flattery and sentimental exhortations of the early socialist writers had been attractive before 1848; the harder but, in the last analysis, not less hopeful, moral and inspiring doctrines of Proudhon[1] were much better suited to a generation only too well aware that the men of 1848 had let their feelings run away with them.

Vacherot's *La Démocratie* and Jules Simon's *La Liberté* (1859) were books as eagerly read in their day as Proudhon's *De la Justice dans la Révolution*. These three works, more than any others, launched the renewed intellectual offensive of the republicans. They were directly critical and therefore disturbing to the régime.

[1] Some French philosophers have been "materialists," but not those who have greatly influenced the French people. Like Pascal, Fénelon, Voltaire, Rousseau, Saint-Simon and Fourier, Proudhon was at heart a moralist, a severe critic of society and an admirer of courage and intellectual honesty.

There were also other books, less concerned with contemporary society but not always less dangerous in the long run. Edgar Quinet published a history of the first revolution, in which he defended the Girondins and attacked the Jacobins. His book was an answer to Michelet's great history of the same revolution proclaiming his admiration for Robespierre and the Mountain. It revived a discussion that must be uncomfortable for an absolute government, a discussion between persons whose every assumption was a condemnation of Bonapartism. Michelet's history was published between 1847 and 1851, and of all histories of the revolution written in the nineteenth century it had the greatest influence on the republican and popular cause. Michelet spoke of the "people" as of a force mysterious and formidable, always present and yet not always seen, always just and yet seldom easily understood. He thought of the people as the great actor of history, protean and heroic, difficult to identify, inarticulate and unpredictable, simple, profound and endowed with all the virtues. Patience, simplicity, courage, fortitude, magnanimity and wisdom —the combination of qualities that unusual strength of mind and moral discipline give to perhaps one man in ten thousand—he ascribed to the people. He was the inspired idolator of his age and country. The idol he made was the most impressive image of the great hero of the republicans, the hero called "people," for whose sake they made their sacrifices according to the measure of their courage and devotion.

The intellectuals of France were at last beginning to take notice of German philosophy. The study of Kant, and the neo-Kantian movement that resulted from it, made more exacting and austere the discussion of social and moral questions. Littré and the positivists, though their philosophy was much more in the French tradition, had something the same effect on the intellectual life of France. It became the fashion to be unsentimental, learned, philosophical (whether harshly metaphysical or aggressively positivist), hostile to religion and the church, to look twice at everything except your own assumptions, to be severely critical and icily dogmatic. Some writers even began to bully or stun or overwhelm their readers with their learning, as if tact and taste and elegance were qualities that Frenchmen needed no longer. Recent and striking progress had been made in the biological sciences; and now historians and other students of men and society were eager that they too should be scientists.

This burst of intellect was too much even for the Blanquists, who fell victims to the prevailing mood and thought it their duty to justify their existence. Their philosopher or historian (it does not much matter which) was Tridon, whose book on the *Hébertistes* appeared in 1863. The Blanquists praised the Jacobins for their strength and courage, but condemned their indifference to social problems. They praised the Commune of 1794 and exalted Paris above the rest of France. The great mistake of the democrats, according to Tridon, was their contempt for force, their respect for legality. The revolution must be made for France by Paris, by the most advanced and intelligent part of the nation.

All this intellectual ferment excited the Latin Quarter, where, one after another, many small newspapers made an appearance, lasted a little while and then died out. Some ten of them were more important than the others, especially *l'Avenir* to which Vacherot contributed articles, Vermorel's three papers, *Le Travail* for which Clémenceau and Zola wrote, and Charles Longuet's *Rive Gauche*, the first French newspaper to expound the Marxist doctrine. Longuet was himself still a Proudhonist, but he allowed Lafargue to write a series of articles explaining Marxism.

In 1859 the Emperor granted a general and unconditional amnesty to the republican exiles. Most of them took advantage of it, except Ledru-Rollin who was not covered by it and Louis Blanc who stayed abroad until 1870. This concession was soon followed by others in 1860, when decrees were published allowing the *Corps Législatif* to publish its debates, to present addresses and to propose amendments. These concessions were more important than they looked; they enabled the republicans in the legislature to make a better show of opposing the government and to publish their opposition to the people. The republicans felt more effective and more hopeful; they were less tempted than they had been to make plots. Revolutionary action, so frequent and so useless from 1852 to 1859, was now almost abandoned. Blanqui, of course, who, like all other political prisoners, was let free when the general amnesty was granted, could not keep quiet. He plotted violence and in June 1861 was brought to trial once more and afterwards sent to prison. Only a few workers were implicated with him. The next year there was another trial for conspiracy, when fifty-four persons, mostly returned exiles, were accused of plotting to kidnap the Emperor. The evidence at both these trials was weak, and yet it was the best the police could do to show that the republicans and socialists still believed in violence.

Napoleon, during these middle years of his reign, was in an awkward position. His Italian policy offended the church. Though he prevented the Italians from taking Rome, it was he who had made possible the united Italy that now coveted Rome. While he protected what remained of the papal dominions, the church would not abandon the Emperor; but she had lost faith in him. Napoleon felt that he must look for support outside the church. It was not enough that the peasant masses should accept his rule and vote as he wanted them to. The peasants were formidable as enemies but not as friends. Outside the church there was only one moral force in France of major political importance. That force was republicanism. The Emperor was not deceived by the small number of votes cast for the republicans at the last elections. He knew too much about the management of elections to make that mistake. The republicans were strong though it was still impossible for them to display their strength. Napoleon did not want to share power with them, but he wanted to make them better disposed to himself, in case he should need their alliance later. He thought it wiser to make political life just tolerable to them.

Some of Napoleon's advisers, men like Morny, Persigny and Prince Napoleon, wanted him to make a bid for liberal and republican support. Indeed, his cousin, Prince Napoleon, the most radical member of the imperial family, had a notion that the Emperor could, if he wished, win over the urban workers. A paternal interest in people who had suffered so much in the revolutionary cause and gained so little from it might make allies where they were least expected. The workers, after all, were the fighting wing of the republican movement. They were well worth conciliating, and with such poor people a little help might go a long way. It was not a bad idea, and the Prince also had better motives for his interest in the workers.

Other friends of the Emperor, his Foreign Minister, Walewski, his Chief of Police, Rouher, and above all his wife, advised him to maintain absolute government and the Catholic alliance. No concessions to the republicans, short of the abdication of power, if not of the throne, would satisfy them. One concession, they thought, must follow another until all was lost. But if the Emperor remained absolute, the clergy would not abandon him, knowing as they did that it was he alone who could keep the Italians out of Rome. Napoleon could not make up his mind what advice to follow. He wanted to remain all-powerful himself and yet be able to rely on the support of powerful friends. The obstinacy and ingratitude of the church annoyed him, but he could not bring himself to make enemies of the clergy. On the other hand, he dared not take away from the republicans what he had so recently given them. He had paid too small a price to buy their friendship, and yet, if he took back what he had paid, they would hate him worse than ever. He did not know what to do. He moved, or looked as if he intended to move, now in one direction and now in the other. He felt his weakness and others soon felt it too. The passive support of the great majority of the nation could not make it up to him for the church's distrust and the republicans' hostility and contempt.

Republican opposition to the Empire was clandestine and revolutionary until 1857; and until 1863 it was more cultural and intellectual than political. Opposition became primarily political only in 1863, when the republicans, in spite of the system of official candidatures, triumphed in Paris at the general election. They won eight of the seats in the capital, the ninth (and only other) going to Thiers, also an opponent of the Empire. Some seven and a quarter million voters went to the polls, of whom 5,300,000 voted for the official candidates and nearly two millions for the opposition. There were at that time in France twenty-two towns with over forty thousand inhabitants, and in only four of them (Rouen, Angers, Strasbourg and Orleans) did the government poll more votes than the opposition. Some of Napoleon's opponents were royalists, but the bulk of them were republicans. In the towns, the apparent strength of republicanism was already as great as it had ever been; and its apparent strength, since all the dice were loaded in favour of the government, was presumably smaller than its real strength.

The election results shocked the Emperor[1] and his advisers. Morny and Prince Napoleon thought the time had come to move swiftly towards a parliamentary and liberal régime. The church, they said, was offended and unforgiving. Her priests still advised the peasants to vote for the official candidates, but her high dignitaries were severely critical of the Emperor's Italian policy and were inclined to sell their support too dearly. The future was with the parties of the left. It was better to make concessions with a good grace now than be obliged to make them later. But the Empress and Rouher were not less firm on the other side. Only the Emperor could keep the Italians out of Rome; he was therefore as necessary to the church as she to him. Besides, the republicans and socialists were now, more ardently than ever before, enemies of the church and even of religion. The republicans were more dangerous to the church than to the Emperor, who must now protect her against anti-clericals, free-thinkers and atheists. Both groups of advisers spoke the truth to Napoleon. But they also forgot circumstances that must make either choice seem dangerous to him. Was it possible to repress the republicans for ever? Could he rule France indefinitely, through his police and army, and enjoying only a luke-warm friendship with the church? On the other hand, if he gave the republicans the freedom they asked for, how long would they put up with him? Some of them, like Émile Ollivier and Darimon, had watched his vacillations with sympathy; but the others, leaders having greater authority, were irreconcilable. Napoleon continued to hesitate until January 1867, when he summoned Ollivier to him and told him he had decided to make the Empire liberal. He must, he said, be allowed to do so gradually, that it might not appear as if he were acting from weakness. Progress towards a liberal régime was slow indeed, and it took three more years to transform the Empire into a parliamentary and democratic monarchy.

Meanwhile, the republicans, the royalists and Prince Napoleon were all competing for the favour of the workers. The thing to do, they all said, was to encourage co-operatives, institutions not

---

[1] A dictator who makes his own use of elections also looks at them in his own way. He is less interested in the votes he gets than in those denied him. In this he is wise, because his tyranny has separated the brave from the docile. He can count more certainly on the hatred of those who defy him than on the loyalty of those who do not.

incompatible with the free economy in which they all believed, and which could, they thought, bring real benefits to the workers. In 1866 the Emperor subscribed half a million francs to a *Fund for Co-operative Societies* and the Prince Imperial 300,000 francs to the Lyon Weavers' Co-operative. Royalists like the duc d'Audriffet-Pasquier and Prince Albert de Broglie wrote pamphlets proving the legality of co-operatives. The republicans ran at least three newspapers to encourage the co-operative movement. Autocracy and the police state still survived, but times were greatly altered. Ten years earlier any attempt to organise workers, even for the most innocent purposes, was looked upon as a crime against the state.

Prince Napoleon was especially active on behalf of the workers. Among his friends he counted Armand Lévy, who in his youth had frequented socialist and republican clubs. Since that time he had been a tutor in several noble families and had become respectable. He ran a newspaper, *l'Espérance*, in which he expounded the principles of "national self-determination" and "imperial democracy." In the early sixties he got in touch with some of his old working-class friends and tried to persuade them to form workers' societies which the imperial administration could tolerate. He was not very successful. But just before the World Exhibition to be held in London in the summer of 1862, Lévy persuaded Prince Napoleon that it would be wise to send a workers' delegation to London. It was agreed that a few workers, most of them on the editorial staff of *l'Espérance*, should write two letters, one to the Emperor and the other to the Prince, asking that a workers' delegation be sent to London. The Emperor thought well of the idea and 200,000 francs were put at the disposal of the delegates, who were to be chosen by the workers themselves. About two hundred workers went to London; and it was on the occasion of their visit that it was first suggested to establish an international working men's association. When the French delegates returned from London, they immediately broke off relations with Prince Napoleon.

The next year (1864) some French workers' delegates, this time quite independently of the government, again went to London to attend a meeting of protest against Russia's treatment of the Poles. On September 26th, 1864, at a meeting held in St. Martin's Hall, the Frenchmen formally proposed the creation of an *International Association of Working Men*. The proposal was adopted and a committee chosen to draft a constitution for the new society. The rules of the association, and especially the preamble to them, were inspired by Karl Marx, one of the members of the constituent committee. But at that time there was little more in common between the workers who joined the association than the belief that working men all over the world should co-operate to improve the lot of their class. Not one in ten of the delegates who met in London in 1864 knew how the doctrines of Marx differed from those of any other socialist.

The Paris section of the first International at once registered with the authorities. This act and the benevolent attitude of the police made the International suspect to the Blanquists and more extreme republicans. Yet the leaders of the Paris section were from the first politically republican, and they published their notices and opinions in the republican press. The benevolence of the police was soon exhausted because the Paris section obstinately refused to accept imperial patronage.

At first the International made slow progress in France, but the effective help given by the Paris section to the bronze-workers, when they went on strike in February 1867, astonished and pleased the workers throughout the country. Tolain, the most prominent member of the Paris section, went to London to collect money for the strikers. The employers, frightened by this unprecedented example of international working-class solidarity, immediately gave in to the strikers. This great victory caused tens of thousands of workers to join the International. As soon as the workers anywhere decided to strike, their society, whether old-established or formed for the occasion, asked to join the International. As strikes multiplied so too did the great association, until in 1870 it had already a quarter of a million members in France.

The International, at its early conferences in Geneva and Lausanne, where French and Swiss delegates were in the majority, passed resolutions that favoured workers' co-operatives. Not till September 1868, at the Brussels Conference, were the majority of the delegates collectivists, but on that occasion the French and Swiss were outnumbered. The French sections of the first International never became predominantly collectivist. During the first trial of the leaders of the Paris section of the International at the end of 1867, a new bureau was elected to take their place. Tolain and his friends, then standing their trial, were Proudhonists; their successors, especially Varlin, the most energetic of them, were collectivists. As the bureau of the Paris section of the International was incomparably more important than any other in France, this change of leaders was certainly important. But it did not make the Paris section collectivist, and still less the other sections. The French workers were going on strike more frequently than ever. What they expected and got from the International was help quickly given in their need. They were more concerned to get this help than to dispute about theory. Most of them probably were Proudhonists still, at least in this vague sense: that they believed society ought to be transformed, the over-mighty state destroyed, and as much freedom as possible left to the workers. Their neglect of theory did no harm to the French sections of the International. They prospered, and their prosperity alarmed the government. There were two more trials of leaders of the International, in 1868 and 1870, before the Second Empire collapsed.

III. THE EMPIRE BAITED AND MAULED

The International, whatever the resolutions of its conferences abroad, was always in France less doctrinaire than practical. It was not popular with the other republican and socialist organisations. The moderate republicans, at first friendly to it, were soon afraid that it would frighten the middle classes and throw them into the arms of the Emperor. The Blanquists despised an association more interested in supporting strikers than promoting revolution. The Jacobins, still loyal to the traditions of 1793, though they called themselves social reformers, were more interested in politics.

From 1867 until the abdication of the Emperor, the republican opposition, in the legislature, in the press, and at public meetings, increased in confidence, severity and volume. From March 1868, the censorship was relaxed, permission to hold public meetings

more easily obtained and deputies allowed to interpellate ministers. The violent language of the press and of speakers at public
meetings soon caused the police to prosecute offenders as often
as the milder laws would allow. But though the authorities,
disappointed in their hopes, dealt with the republicans as severely
as they could, the concessions once granted were never with-
drawn. The radical press in the capital, especially Delescluze in
Le Réveil and Henri de Rochefort in *La Lanterne* and then in *La
Marseillaise*, insulted the government and the imperial family in
a manner never seen before except in time of revolution. The
police and the army could still maintain law and order; the
peasants were still docile and the church not unfriendly; the
foundations of the régime still appeared solid. But men needed
to remind themselves of these facts to believe in the security of
the Empire. If they forgot them and looked only at what was
happening in Paris, in the large towns and industrial areas, they
might well conclude that the days of the Empire were numbered.

There were innumerable groups of republicans hostile to the
Emperor. They never formed a solid opposition. If we look not
so much at their organisations and the alliances between them as
at the general tendency of their actions, we can distinguish five
main types of republicans. First of all, inside the legislature, there
were the *Gauche Ouverte* and the *Gauche Fermée*, each with supporting newspapers, publicists and organisations outside parliament. To the *Gauche Ouverte* belonged the most moderate of
moderate republicans, men who were willing to co-operate with
the régime for specific purposes, but who could not, like Émile
Ollivier, bring themselves to believe that the Empire could ever
be truly liberal. They therefore remained firmly opposed in
principle to every kind of monarchy. Their moderation made
them attractive to former Orleanists, men like Thiers, who
thought parliamentary government could never be safe while a
Bonaparte was on the throne, and also, now that manhood
suffrage had come to stay, that a Bourbon restoration was no
longer possible. These men already believed what Thiers was to
say a few years later, that the republic would divide Frenchmen
least.

The *Gauche Fermée* were a more mixed bag. They got their
name for refusing to co-operate with the imperial government on

K

any terms. Some of them were very moderate republicans like
Jules Simon who could not get over their dislike of everything
connected with the man of December. Others, also quite moderate at heart, found it easier to work with the Jacobins and
socialists. The ablest of them all was Gambetta, always further
to the left in his words than his actions. He and those who
thought like him called themselves social reformers, but they
never knew what exactly it was they wanted to do for the workers.
The majority of republicans in France supported one or other of
these two groups. The principles they stood for were these:
personal liberty, parliamentary government, equality of opportunity, dislike of every sort of police or administrative pressure,
anti-clericalism, and suspicion of the army. These were not quite
the same as the principles of the moderates of 1848. Manhood
suffrage existed already. Anti-clericalism and dislike of the
professional army were much stronger now than they had been
twenty years before. So, too, was the belief in social reform. It is
absurd to say, as some people have done, that that belief meant
nothing, because neither the *Gauche Ouverte* or *Fermée* had a
detailed programme of social reform. To say openly that such
reforms are necessary is to admit the duty of society to the poor.
Such an admission, repeatedly and openly made by so large a
party, is always important. If the Third Republic did so little for
the workers during the early decades of its life, it was only because
it had first to establish itself against the royalists and to live down
the memory of the Commune. The leaders of the *Gauche Ouverte*
and the *Gauche Fermée*, who were later to take over the government of the republic from the conservatives, were opposed to the
Commune of 1871 from the moment of its appearance.

To the left of these two groups, the only ones considerably
represented in the legislature, there were three others: the
Jacobins, the Blanquists and the French sections of the International. The Jacobins of the late sixties were in several respects
different from their predecessors of the second republic. They
were more extreme than the radicals who had made so many
converts to republicanism between 1849 and 1851. Most of the
provincial converts of those years now took their lead from men
like Gambetta. The Jacobins of the late sixties were almost confined to the great towns, and were especially strong in Paris. The

coup d'état of 1851 and the police régime of Louis Napoleon had convinced them that France must be decentralised, that the smallest administrative units, the communes, must be strong, and the largest, the state, as weak as possible. Manhood suffrage and parliamentary government were, they thought, clearly not enough. Louis Napoleon had shown that he could use both to become absolute master of France. The Jacobins, more defiant than they had ever been, wanted to abolish the army, to substitute for it a citizen militia and to establish a single progressive income tax. They also loudly clamoured for social reform, and it was this that reconciled to them such men as Raspail, who could not share their admiration for Robespierre and the Mountain. The best known of the Jacobins, Delescluze and Rochefort, were the most popular journalists in Paris. When the regular French armies were defeated by the Prussians, they wanted the war fought through to a finish, confident that raw levies would again save the republic from the Prussians as they had done nearly eighty years before. Delescluze and Rochefort both supported the Commune.

The French sections of the International were the least revolutionary of the three groups on the extreme left. Their leaders tried unsuccessfully to form a workers' parliamentary party. Their only candidate at the elections of 1869 was defeated. The workers wanted help from the International in their trade disputes, but for political leadership they looked elsewhere. The leaders of the French sections were, in any case, unable to offer them strong guidance; they were divided in their allegiance to the rival principles of collectivism and co-operation. The leaders of the Paris sections did, however, take a prominent part in the Commune.

The Blanquists were still the only professed revolutionaries. Other people may have believed in the class war as a matter of theory, but the Blanquists alone believed that insurrectionary methods could succeed in the France of 1867 to 1870. The Blanquists were by this time avowed communists; they believed in community of property. But they still had no opinions about how communism should be established in contemporary France. Their energies were all devoted to making a successful revolution. They still believed in the immense superiority of Paris over the rest of France, and of the towns over the villages. They therefore cared nothing for "abstract" democracy. The defeat of the workers in June 1848 had taught them that a highly centralised administration no longer enabled Paris to dominate France. Their great concern now was that France should not be allowed to stifle progress in Paris. They, too, like the Jacobins, had become champions of decentralisation. When a revolutionary Commune was established in 1871 in Paris they were quite perfectly in their element.

At the last parliamentary elections of the Second Empire, in May 1869, the opposition polled 3,350,000 votes to the government's 4,438,000. Most of the opposition votes went to the republicans, who triumphed as absolutely in Paris as the government did in the more backward provinces. The Emperor, if he had any doubts before, now knew it was too late to turn back. The decree of September 6th, 1869, giving the *Corps Législatif* the right to initiate laws and the unlimited right to interpellate ministers, virtually re-established parliamentary government. Napoleon still seemed to hesitate; until the end of the year he governed France through ministers who did not enjoy the confidence of the legislature. But on December 27th he made his last concession; he invited Émile Ollivier to form a government. On January 2nd, 1870, France became the only democratic parliamentary monarchy among the great powers. But Napoleon could not hope to become popular with the republicans. They could never forgive him, though they might, when the time came, decide not to visit on his son the sins of the father. His dynasty might yet survive; and that must be hope enough for a sick man. Unfortunately, within a few months of the final establishment of the liberal empire, France was caught up in a disastrous war with Prussia.

Chapter Six

THE PARIS COMMUNE

I. PARIS QUARRELS WITH FRANCE

ON September 4th, three days after the Emperor's capitulation at Sedan, the third Republic was proclaimed in Paris. The crowd invaded the legislature and carried off the republican deputies to the Town Hall, and at six o'clock that evening, the Government of National Defence was established. The new government of six members (Favre, Simon, Ferry, Trochu, Picard and Rochefort) consisted, with one exception (Rochefort) of moderate republicans. It was not a case, as it had been in 1848, of Paris newspapers and leaders popular in the capital outside parliament taking power. Rochefort was the only member of the new government really popular with the more extreme republicans and the workers of the capital. But Rochefort was isolated and felt his weakness inside the government. He could exercise no influence on the others. He was not the sort of man who knew how to gain the confidence of his colleagues and win concessions from them. He was, from the beginning, hostile to the government he belonged to; if he were ever to be powerful, it must be in spite of them.

The radical wing of the republicans soon learnt to distrust the new government. The Federal Council of Paris Sections of the International, together with other radical bodies, formed on September 11th the *Central Committee of the Twenty Districts*[1] of Paris. Each district had been invited to set up a committee, and each committee to send four delegates to the Central Committee. The men who promoted this scheme intended that the committee should watch and stimulate the municipal governments, while the Central Committee did the same by the Government of National

---

[1] I refer, of course, to the *arrondissements*.

Defence. The *Central Committee* was at first not hostile to the new government, but merely suspicious. Its establishment did, however, prove that the more extreme republicans, the leaders whose power and popularity were greatest in Paris, did not trust the moderates. Not all the Jacobins and revolutionaries supported the Central Committee. Many of them, like Blanqui, Delescluze, Pyat and Flourens, disliked the International so much that they would have nothing to do with committees sponsored by it. They did not, however, think any the better of the Government of National Defence on that account. They attacked it in their newspapers and in their club: Blanqui in *La Patrie en danger*, Delescluze in *Le Réveil* and Pyat in *Le Combat*.

France was at war. Both the *Central Committee* and the Jacobins and revolutionaries who kept away from it were interested above all in the conduct of the war. The connexion between their hostility to the government, whom they accused of inefficiency, and the military situation is made clear by the dates of the two insurrections before the armistice of January 28th. On October 30th, news of Bazaine's capitulation at Metz reached Paris. The next day there was an insurrection, when the Jacobins and Blanquists captured the Town Hall and proclaimed a new government. Flourens, Pyat, Delescluze and Blanqui all belonged to it. In imitation of the Convention, they formed a *Committee of Public Safety* and they announced that a Commune would be established in Paris as soon as possible. The insurgents were not long in possession of the Town Hall. Several legions of the National Guard and two Breton battalions stationed in Paris drove them out and reinstated the Government of National Defence. The insurgent leaders were promised an amnesty, but some slight evidence that they were still plotting an insurrection was taken by the government as an excuse for not keeping their promise. Yet the Government of National Defence also owed their power to an act of violence, to the insurrection of September 4th; they had no better right to govern France than the insurgents of October 31st. Their proceedings against the latter did them no good. Blanqui escaped, the evidence against Pyat and Delescluze was found insufficient, and Flourens, who had led the insurrection, was not captured till December. The Government of National Defence were proving mean and ineffective: they had decided to punish others for doing what they had done themselves, and then had found it impossible to punish them.

The insurrection of October 31st did, however, have one result unforeseen by either party to the quarrel. The *Central Committee of the Twenty Districts* ceased to exist, and the men who had created it drifted into the Jacobin and Blanquist clubs, whose membership rapidly increased. The insurrection had failed but it had not weakened opposition to the government; on the contrary, it had made it more united than before. The government, to recover their prestige and to acquire the legal status they so badly wanted, organised a plebiscite in Paris on November 3rd. Five hundred and fifty thousand persons voted for the government and only sixty thousand against them. But plebiscites are notoriously misleading; they seldom offer the voters a choice of alternatives, and are often merely invitations to accept an accomplished fact. The municipal elections of November 4th are better evidence of how the Parisians felt about their government and the conduct of the war. In seventeen out of twenty districts candidates supporting the government were elected; the opposition carried only the eighteenth, nineteenth and twentieth, the most proletarian districts in the capital. There was perhaps not much love anywhere for the Government of National Defence, but most Parisians still thought it their duty to vote for them in face of the Prussian invasion.

The second insurrection happened on January 22nd, three days after the disastrous sortie of the Paris National Guard towards Buzenval. A few radical battalions of the National Guard assembled outside the Town Hall and sent in a deputation to demand the immediate election of a communal assembly in Paris. Their demand was refused. Some of the National Guardsmen then began to fire at the regular troops inside the Town Hall, who returned their fire. The National Guard battalions and the crowd that had collected around them were soon dispersed, leaving about fifty dead behind them. The government, after the insurrection, took more drastic action against the extreme left. Several political clubs were closed down, and two important newspapers, Delescluze's *Le Réveil* and Pyat's *Le Combat*, were suppressed. Six days after this second insurrection, on January 28th, 1871, the 135th day of the siege of Paris, Bismarck granted an armistice to France. The French were to elect a National Assembly to decide whether or not the war was to be continued; they were also obliged to surrender the forts defending Paris and to disarm all their regular troops except twelve thousand men. But they were not required to disarm the National Guard. The armistice, whatever the intentions of the men who negotiated it, by depriving her of her armies, made it impossible for France to continue the war. On the other hand, it left in existence an armed force, the National Guard, which, though too weak to resist the Prussians, was strong enough, should it feel so inclined, to defy any French government.

Napoleon III had had no use for the National Guard and had reduced it almost to nothing. It had been revived after his abdication. The quick victories of the Prussians had destroyed the prestige of the regular army. On September 6th, two days after the fall of the Empire, the Government of National Defence authorised the formation of sixty battalions of the National Guard, battalions that were not intended to maintain order but to fight the enemy. Instead of sixty battalions there were soon formed one hundred and ninety-four, a great army of about three hundred thousand men. Everyone who could joined the National Guard, either from patriotism or to avoid starvation. Unemployment in Paris during the siege was so great that the 1f. 50c. a day received by every National Guardsman was all that stood between most working-class families and complete penury.

During the July Monarchy and the Second Republic, the National Guard had been a middle-class army. Every guardsman had provided his own equipment, and this single requirement had kept the workers out. But in 1870 the National Guard was revived for the defence of Paris. The guardsmen were no longer required to equip themselves; on the contrary, they even received a daily wage. The National Guard in 1870 was to the workers of Paris what the National Workshops had been in 1848. It was their daily bread. It was also much more. It was their army and their contribution to the defence of the republic. The most radical battalions were the most warlike and made the greatest noise. They asked for and got the best equipment that could be supplied to them. Not all the battalions were radical, but as the siege continued, the temper of the National Guardsmen changed. On

October 31st, several battalions had been willing to defend the government and the others had not intervened. By the end of January their mood was no longer the same. By that time there were more proletarian battalions properly armed, battalions more radical and more hostile to the government. Semi-starvation, long periods of inaction, and, at last, the disastrous failure of a sortie long awaited and yet badly prepared; all this, and the bad news from the provinces showing that the new armies raised by Gambetta were no match for the Prussians, exasperated the Parisians and the great majority of the National Guard. They accused the government of incompetence, cowardice and treachery. On January 22nd, battalions of the National Guard had dared to fire at the Town Hall, the seat of the government. They had been easily dispersed because the regulars had fired back at them. They had hoped to force the government to concede their demands, but they had not wanted, with the Prussians surrounding Paris, to precipitate a civil war. And now the armistice was taking all the regular troops out of the capital, leaving the National Guard in undisputed military control. The battalions recruited from the wealthier districts were still loyal to the government and to the Assembly that replaced it. But the proletarian battalions, more numerous and more aggressive, felt they owed nothing to a government and an Assembly that were about to betray France.

The siege and the armistice had put Paris out of temper with the rest of France. The Parisians felt they had not been defeated. They had resisted the Prussians for over four months and were willing still to resist them. It was the provincials who had been defeated, and it was the provincials, dominated by the church and the bourgeois, who had supported the Second Empire. They were unpatriotic and reactionary, and because of them all the great sacrifices of the Parisians had been made in vain. This was the mood of the Parisians in January and February 1871. They were nervous, exhausted, angry, defiant and full of their own virtues. Many of the richer citizens had fled from the capital before the siege began and others had moved out quickly as soon as it was over. This flight of the wealthy exasperated the poor, and it also made them stronger. Paris was now more entirely theirs than she had ever been, and they had proved the only citizens worthy of her. Fatigue, anger and despair put the Parisians somewhat out of their minds. They did not want peace and yet they knew no better than anyone else how the war might be continued. They had no thought of fighting alone; their forts were now occupied by the Prussians and they knew they could not force their will on France. They could not even cut themselves off from France. The ties that bound them to her were indissoluble and yet they would not acknowledge them. They did not know what they wanted but were resolved not to be put upon. They were sore and could bear only the gentlest touch.

The elections for the National Assembly took place in Paris on February 5th and in the provinces on February 8th. Of the forty-three deputies elected in the Seine department, ten (including Pyat, Delescluze, Malon and Rochefort) were later to become members of the Commune; and of the other thirty-three nearly all were republicans and many were Jacobins. But in the provinces, except in the large towns, the royalists were everywhere successful, not because the French people liked monarchy but because there was no other way of voting for peace. The Bonapartists were discredited and the republicans were the war party. The provinces wanted an immediate peace, while Paris was for the continuance of war.

The new Assembly offended Paris not only by its pacifism but also in other ways. Indeed, the Parisians, though they might not be willing to admit it, must have known that it was impossible, the armistice terms once accepted, to make war on the Prussians. If they had had no other grievances, if they had been treated more tactfully, they might have accepted the inevitable, with a bad grace, no doubt, and yet without civil war. The Parisians, in the mood they were in after the long siege they had endured, deserved to be treated gently, to be humoured a little and led quietly where they would have in the end in any case to go. But the Assembly either did not understand how the Parisians felt or else thought it a weakness to indulge them. Some of the things done could not have been avoided. The triumphal march of the Prussians through Paris, though it was felt as a humiliation after a four months' siege, was a concession made to Bismarck for a greater gain elsewhere. The appointment of Thiers as Chief of the Executive, though it offended the Parisians, was perhaps inevitable. He was the only French statesman with a European reputation; he was an enemy of Napoleon III and he was on good terms both with the moderate republicans and the royalists. Thiers was hated by the Jacobins and the revolutionaries. He had suppressed the workers' insurrection in Lyon in 1834, and he had led the *Parti de l'Ordre*, the conservatives, in 1848. The Parisians—or rather the men who now dominated Paris—were offended by the mere thought of him. His appointment added to their fears and suspicions; and yet, in the circumstances, it was perhaps the only appointment the Assembly could have made. Also offensive to the Parisians, though equally justifiable on other grounds, was the decision made by the Assembly to move from Bordeaux to Versailles and not to Paris. The deputies, knowing how often in the past the Jacobins and revolutionaries in the capital had imposed their will on a sovereign Assembly, were perfectly entitled to choose to sit in a town where they could deliberate without fear of the mob.

But other things done by the Assembly and by Thiers were deeply offensive to the Parisians without being either necessary or just. On March 3rd, General d'Aurelles de Paladines, a man thoroughly disliked by the Parisians, was appointed commander of the National Guard in Paris. The Jacobins thought him a reactionary and his appointment the prelude to the disbanding of the National Guard. At about this time, too, a Military Court sentenced Flourens and Blanqui to death for their part in the insurrection of October 31st. These men had used force to overthrow a government established by force, and the sentence passed on them seemed to the radicals a deliberate provocation, an act of class war. The Assembly made other mistakes more gross than these. On March 11th it passed the *Law of Maturities*. In August 1870 the dates at which all financial obligations fell due had been postponed. The new law made them all payable within a short time. And the Assembly also announced a measure providing for the collection of rents not paid during the siege. Shopkeepers and artisans who had done almost no business for several months, who had stayed in Paris while their creditors had fled to safety and good food, suddenly found themselves liable to pay their debts within a few weeks or months. Working men who had eaten very little food for a hundred days were now to be required to pay back rent to persons many of whom had left Paris long before the siege began. The *Law of Maturities* and the announcement about rents were cruel and stupid blunders; they convinced the Parisians that the deputies were their enemies, inspired by the meanest and most vindictive motives. Indeed, the *Law of Maturities*, affecting not so much the workers as the lower middle class, gave friends to the proletariat without whose help they could hardly have defied the Assembly for two whole months.

All through February and March the temper of the Parisians and the Assembly was rising. The Jacobins and revolutionaries in the capital had by this time established their control over the National Guard. Early in February, there emerged the Federation of the National Guard, with a central committee of elected delegates to act in the name of the entire citizen militia of Paris. Leaders of the Paris sections of the International were well represented on this Central Committee, but it never became socialist. The committee was originally formed to endorse candidates for the elections of February 5th. This it did in agreement with the Montagnard Club, the International and several other bodies. The Federation and the Central Committee continued to exist after the elections, because the delegates from the battalions of the National Guard liked the organisation they had formed and thought it might be useful to them in the future. The limits of its authority were never defined and were never known to anyone, but until the election of the Commune on March 28th it was the body in Paris most representative of the opponents of Thiers and the Assembly. The election of the Commune diminished its importance but did not reduce it to insignificance. It still claimed authority in the military sphere and received some obedience. The Central Committee of the National Guard was never an effective body but its emergence was nevertheless decisive. For some important time it alone could speak for about two hundred battalions of the National Guard, and also for every kind of socialist, revolutionary and radical in Paris. Though its policy was hesitant and its authority obscure, it was the earliest spokesman of the insurgents. As the power of this committee increased, it became more and more evident that Paris had decided to defy France.

II. THE REVOLT OF PARIS

Thiers knew that his own and the Assembly's policy was exasperating the already irritable Parisians. He decided that it would be wise to disarm the National Guard. He could not, of course, take their rifles from them, for that would have involved a house-to-house search and precipitated an insurrection before the insurgents could be disarmed. He thought he would do well enough if he could deprive the Parisians of their guns. The guns in question had been paid for by public subscriptions, and the citizens thought of them not as the property of the state but their own. When the Prussians were due to march through the capital, the Parisians had hauled their guns away into the working-class districts to prevent their falling into the hands of the enemy. Thiers' purpose was now to retrieve them.

On the night of March 17th–18th he sent fifteen thousand troops and three thousand police into Paris to seize these guns and take them out of the city as quietly as they could. The attempt ought to have succeeded. The guns were not defended and they could have been hauled away quite easily while the National Guardsmen were in their beds. The attempt could not, of course, have passed unnoticed, but if the troops had moved quickly enough they could have been out of Paris before the National Guard had had time to muster an effective resistance. Though the National Guardsmen in Paris greatly outnumbered the troops and police sent in by Thiers, and in their own city could fight the intruders on more than equal terms, they were always slow to assemble, and the troops could hope to be out of the narrow streets before anyone had had time to erect a barricade.

Unfortunately for Thiers the adventure was mismanaged. When the troops had seized the guns, they found they had not enough horses, ropes and harnesses for their purpose. Before they were ready to move off with their booty, the sun had risen and the National Guard had been warned. Crowds of civilians and National Guardsmen surrounded the troops and coaxed or frightened many of them into deserting their officers. Those who did not desert were soon too few to offer the least resistance, and they were allowed to go quietly out of the capital. Thiers' discomfiture was complete. It was an attempt which, if it did not succeed, could only fail ignominiously.

During the morning of March 18th, two generals, Lecomte and Clément-Thomas, were taken prisoner. The National Guard took them for safe-keeping into a house. The mob later invaded the house and shot the generals out of hand. Neither the local command of the National Guard nor the Central Committee were responsible for these murders. They were done by a mob brought together by chance and instigated by no one knows whom. All this, however, was not known at the time. When Thiers and the Assembly heard of these crimes, they did not doubt they were the deliberate acts of the National Guard, gestures of defiance against the legal government of France. The expedition that had failed and the murder of the generals hardened men's hearts and closed their minds. There had already been talk of civil war; but men had spoken of it only as something that was possible. They had continued to hope, and had good reasons to hope, it might be avoided. After all, what had the Parisians to gain by their obstinacy, or Thiers and the Assembly by their harshness? Men's nerves were frayed and their tempers bad long before March 18th, but until that day it had always seemed possible and even likely that in the end both parties would see they had nothing to gain by violence. But now there was little hope that reason would prevail, though men of good will might still attempt a reconciliation. Both sides prepared for a battle that neither side, before March 18th, had really wanted. And the Parisians, neither then nor at any other time while the battle lasted, knew exactly what it was they were fighting for.

After the failure of his expedition, Thiers decided to evacuate the capital. He had only a small number of troops at his disposal and he could not—as what had happened on the morning of March 18th proved—rely on them. He thought it wise to wait until he could raise a reliable army; and that he could not do without the permission of Bismarck. So Thiers repeated in 1871 what he had done at Lyon in 1834; he allowed the insurgents a few days' grace before he set about destroying them. Some people have said that Thiers wanted to provoke an insurrection to gain the credit of putting it down. That is what he did in 1834, they say, and he did it again thirty-seven years later. But the two cases are not much alike. In 1834 the insurgents at Lyon were weak and only the withdrawal of the troops gave them their chance to become formidable. In 1871 the Parisians, even before Thiers tried to take their guns, were much stronger than he was. He had no alternative but to play for time. He might have been tactful and conciliatory; in fact he was sly and vindictive; and after March 18th he certainly had no wish to prevent bloodshed. The Parisians had defied the legal government of France, they had taken advantage of their country's defeat to make preposterous demands. For the moment, they were too strong to be punished. Thiers' policy was to allow them to extort no important concessions while he remained weak, and to punish them severely as soon as he was strong. He was a man lacking sympathy for poverty and distress, ungenerous, immodest and self-righteous; but he was also a patriotic Frenchman and the ablest politician in the country.

After March 18th, the Central Committee of the National Guard decided to take over responsibility for maintaining law and order in Paris until a municipal assembly could be elected. Jules Ferry, the mayor of Paris, and most of the authorities left the city; only the district mayors remained behind. They, however, had not the power to govern effectively. The Central Committee assumed responsibility because they alone had power. They had no policy except to maintain order until a municipal assembly was elected. They had not even organised the resistance to Thiers' expedition; indeed, they had known nothing of it until it was over. They were not a revolutionary body but a number of men who found themselves, through no fault of their own, in control of a city that had somehow stumbled into insurrection.[1] But the Central Committee did not act like men whose hand had been forced; their sympathies were altogether with the insurgents. They had not taken the initiative but they were not sorry others had done so. Though they had nothing to do with the resistance successfully offered to Thiers on March 18th, they immediately associated themselves with it. They were happy enough to move

---

[1] On March 19th, the Central Committee controlled all Paris except the first and second districts and parts of the sixth, seventh, ninth and sixteenth districts. The Central Committee could easily have taken over these districts but refrained from doing so until after March 22nd, when the bourgeois still left in Paris organised a demonstration against the insurgents.

in the direction that events were pushing them along. On March 24th the Central Committee repealed the *Law of Maturities*. They borrowed half a million francs from Rothschild, promising to safeguard his interests in Paris, and they also borrowed a million francs from the Bank of France. They got the money they needed to pay the National Guardsmen and so could count on their fidelity.

For several days after March 18th negotiations continued between Thiers and the Central Committee. They were carried on through the good offices of some of the district mayors of Paris and the deputies representing the capital in the National Assembly. The most important of these go-betweens was, perhaps, Georges Clémenceau. A few of the mayors, more hostile to the National Guard than to Versailles, busied themselves organising resistance to the Central Committee in their own districts. The others, more radical in their politics and divided in their sympathies, worked hard for a reconciliation. After the evacuation of Paris by Ferry and most of the authorities, Thiers' Minister of the Interior, Picard, sent a note to the district mayors telling them they were invested with the provisional government of Paris. Real power, of course, belonged to the Central Committee of the National Guard, but the legal authority of the mayors strengthened their hands as negotiators. They decided to send a delegation to the Central Committee.

At the interview between the delegates and the Central Committee, Clémenceau urged the latter to recognise the authority of the National Assembly. They ought, he said, to leave the Town Hall, to hand it over to the district mayors and deputies of Paris, men who were well disposed to the Parisians and were resolved to do their utmost to persuade the Assembly to deal justly with them. Varlin, speaking for the Central Committee, told Clémenceau that they would be satisfied if the Versailles Assembly and government allowed the immediate election of a municipal council, recognised what he called "communal liberties," suppressed the Prefecture of Police, admitted the right of the National Guard to elect their own officers and general commander, made a just law concerning maturities and ordered Vinoy to move his troops twenty leagues from Paris. The Central Committee were then invited in their turn to send delegates to meet the mayors and deputies at the town hall of the second district. At this meeting the more conservative mayors and deputies were present; they probably enjoyed Thiers' confidence and were certainly most unwilling to come to terms with the delegates of the Central Committee. Their hostility did not prevent a compromise: the Paris deputies promised to introduce immediately in the Assembly a bill providing for the election of all National Guard officers and setting up a strong and democratic municipal authority in Paris. In return, the delegates promised that the Central Committee would leave the Town Hall.

The Central Committee at first intended to keep their promise; and they even published posters in the streets of Paris declaring their intention. But the next day, March 21st, they were compelled to change their minds. There had been held a meeting of the Vigilance Committees of the twenty districts, and the Central Committee had been severely criticised for their weakness. Meanwhile, the deputies had introduced their bill to set up a powerful municipal government in Paris, and they had persuaded the Assembly to vote that the bill was urgent. Yet they could not be sure that the Assembly would ever pass the bill. A speech made by Jules Favre violently denouncing the insurgents was received with enthusiasm. In spite of this evidence of the Assembly's hostility to the insurgents, the mayors and deputies, in one of their manifestoes to the Parisians, used language that suggested the bill was unanimously approved by the Assembly. They also invited the Parisians not to vote at the municipal elections illegally decided upon for March 22nd by the Central Committee. The more conservative mayors continued their preparations for eventual resistance to the insurgents, and all the mayors, conservative and radical, refused to hand over to the Central Committee their electoral registers. The Central Committee were therefore obliged to postpone the municipal elections until March 26th.

The demonstration of March 22nd against the Central Committee was organised in the districts still held by the conservative mayors. It started out from the Bourse and ended in the Rue de la Paix, where it was dispersed at the cost of considerable bloodshed. Two days later, on March 24th, the Central Committee captured the town halls of the first and second districts. The day

L

before they had driven Clémenceau out of his offices in the eighteenth district. They were now complete masters of Paris. The position of the mayors and deputies was now more difficult than ever. The insurgents were less persuadable than they had been, while the Assembly and Thiers, in spite of their apparent willingness to make concessions, had still done nothing to satisfy the Parisians. On March 23rd one of the mayors had come to Paris with a letter from Thiers promising that the government would approve any amnesty (*mesures de pardon et d'oubli*) that the mayors might offer to restore order. In another letter, Picard promised that the law setting up a municipal government would be immediately voted, so that elections could be held on April 3rd. But it was also on March 23rd that the Assembly refused to treat as urgent a proposal moved by Arnaud de l'Ariège: "that the Assembly will in future maintain closer relations with the municipalities of Paris and will authorise the mayors to take whatever steps are required by the circumstances; that elections in the National Guard will take place before March 28th and the election of a municipal council before April 3rd." There is no evidence that Thiers was trying to persuade the Assembly to be conciliatory. Yet the messages sent to the mayors by him and by Picard were certainly intended to appease the insurgents. They were also intended to encourage the mayors and deputies of Paris, most of them men of good will anxious to reconcile the two parties to a quarrel that could only weaken France. But Thiers did not want to make terms with the Parisians. They were rebels and must be put down. It may be that some of the mayors shared his opinion and negotiated only to gain time. The others were certainly his dupes; until the municipal elections of March 26th, they believed that Thiers really wanted them to reach a peaceful settlement. Clémenceau, returning to Paris from Versailles on March 25th, had told them the Assembly were opposed to conciliation. This news disturbed the mayors, but they still believed Thiers would support any reasonable compromise and could prevail with the Assembly to accept it. They tried hard to persuade the Central Committee to postpone the municipal elections until after March 26th. When the mayors saw that the Central Committee were determined, whether they liked it or not, to hold the elections on that day, they at last gave in and agreed that they should be held. This "capitulation of the mayors" was later repudiated by the Versaillese. The Parisians, however, thought it authorised by Thiers, and they therefore thought the elections legal. That is why they voted even in the conservative districts. But a day or so after the elections they learned that the mayors' action was repudiated by Thiers, and the representatives of the conservative districts therefore never took their seats in the municipal assembly. About half the electorate voted on March 26th. This, seeing that so many citizens had fled the city before the siege, after the armistice and after March 18th, was a large proportion.

The municipal assembly of Paris, the Commune of 1871, met for the first time on March 28th at the Town Hall. It should have consisted of ninety-one members, but, as six persons were elected to two seats each and the moderates representing the conservative districts never took their seats, the councillors were only about seventy strong at their first meeting. On April 16th supplementary elections were held to fill the twenty-one vacancies. On this later occasion, the proportion of the electors who troubled to vote was extremely small, and this has been put forward as evidence that the Commune had grown quickly unpopular in just over a fortnight. But the supplementary elections were mostly held in the better-to-do districts, whose inhabitants now thought the Commune illegal.[1] That the Commune lost some popularity as it grew older we may well believe; that it lost the support of the classes at first devoted to it is a conclusion not justified by the facts.

As soon as it was installed in the Town Hall, the Commune abolished conscription, ordained that no armed force other than the National Guard should enter Paris, announced that every able-bodied adult male citizen was a member of the National Guard, postponed the payment of rents and debts, and decreed the separation of church and state. These decrees expressed the policy common to all the members of the Commune. There was

[1] On March 26th, 3,732 persons voted in the wealthy sixteenth district, and on April 16th only 1,590. But in the twelfth and eighteenth districts, the figures were respectively: 11,329 (March) falling to 5,423 (April), and 12,442 (March) falling to 10,068 (April). In the nineteenth district, almost wholly proletarian, the figure fell only from 11,282 (March) to 7,090 (April). This last fall is easily accounted for by the smaller interest that electors always take in by-elections. It was on April 16th that the painter Courbet was elected to the Commune.

nothing specifically socialist about any of them. What the Communards wanted was autonomy for Paris and economic security for her citizens. The obligation to pay rents and debts was not repudiated; the claims of property were not in principle rejected. What was done was not done for the sake of a theory, or to injure the rich, but only to give immediate and temporary relief to the poor.

The Commune also set up ten executive committees, of which one, the *Commission Exécutive*, was supposed to be superior to the nine others. These nine committees were responsible for military affairs, security, justice, finance, supply, labour and industry, public services, external relations and education. There was no function of the modern state neglected by the Commune. Yet the powers of these committees were never exactly defined and overlapped considerably. The administration of the Commune was always chaotic. No one ever knew who was responsible for what. Even military operations were not conducted from one centre. The authority of the Military Committee of the Commune was not accepted by the Central Committee of the National Guard. The Central Committee had been eager to expedite the election of the Commune so that responsibility for the general government of Paris might lie with an elected Assembly. But the Central Committee had only wanted to divest themselves of political responsibility; they continued, even after March 28th, to believe that no one had a better right than themselves to direct military operations. They did not deny the authority of the Military Committee; they merely ignored it. The military commanders appointed by the Commune were less fortunate; they found that they could afford to ignore neither the Central nor the Military Committee.

If the insurgents had been properly led, either before March 28th by the Central Committee of the National Guard or afterwards by the Commune, they could have been more formidable than they actually were. They had many advantages. For several weeks their armed forces were greater than those disposed of by Thiers and the Versailles Assembly. They never suffered for lack of money. The Bank of France was in Paris and they were able to borrow nearly fifteen million francs from it. As their entire expenditure was not more than forty millions, they were never threatened with bankruptcy. They had therefore one advantage denied to many legal French governments. Nor did they suffer from lack of food; abundant supplies had been sent quickly into the capital immediately after the armistice. Besides, the Prussians, who still surrounded the greater part of Paris, were quite willing that food should reach the insurgents through their lines. There were profits to be made, and it was to Germany's advantage that France should be torn by civil war. The peasants, of course, were always willing to sell their produce so long as it was paid for in good money. The Parisians were better fed in March, April and May 1871, than they had been during the siege, and they were still paid as regularly as ever. Full employment and a decent wage: the Paris workers had them both for a few months in 1871.

The insurgents had little to fear from the discontented bourgeois left in Paris, especially after the failure of the demonstration of March 22nd. The bourgeois who had not fled the capital were most of them only luke-warm supporters of the Versaillese. They too, like the workers, had been through the siege, and they too had seen men wealthier than themselves leave Paris in good time before the Prussians surrounded it. They might deplore the obstinacy of the Communards; they might believe their enterprise was hopeless; submission to Versailles might seem to them, not only the right, but in the long run the only possible behaviour. Yet they could not, many of them, at least in the early weeks of the insurrection before the hard fighting and the worst atrocities began, help sympathising with the Communards. Most of the prominent supporters of Versailles had in any case left Paris. The friends of "law and order" who remained behind were without leaders and without initiative. They thought it wise to be quiet.

The insurgents, then, had real advantages. And yet they failed to profit by them. They might have marched on Versailles and driven the Assembly and government further into the provinces, or they might even have captured them. They could have occupied the forts and strategic positions outside the capital that were not in Prussian hands. Since they had defied the legal government, it was wisdom to be bold. The odds, in any case and in the long run, were heavily against the insurgents. They could not conquer France; and there was no likelihood, except in a few big towns, that others would follow their example. Their only chance of success—and it was a slender one—was to make themselves as strong as they could and then moderate their demands. Had they appeared both formidable and moderate, the Versaillese might have thought it better to make real concessions to them rather than plunge the country into a prolonged civil war. Or if Thiers and the Assembly had been made prisoners, the Communards might have offered terms to the rest of France that the provincials would have been willing to accept. That was the obvious policy for the Commune: military boldness and political moderation.[1] It might not have succeeded, but nothing else was worth trying.

The insurgents never had a policy, wise or unwise. They made demands, of course, but they did not know how to enforce them, nor what to do to make it worth their enemies' while to concede them. From March 18th to March 28th, what control of the insurrection existed was in the hands of the Central Committee of the National Guard, men whose first wish was to rid themselves of the responsibility thrust upon them by events. They were not exactly afraid of responsibility; they took the blame for whatever happened while they were in control, and they thought it their duty to take responsibility while there was no one else to take it. But they looked upon themselves as caretakers of the people's cause. It was not for them to take the initiative; their business was to carry on till the Parisians could elect a municipal council, and in the meantime to get such a council elected as quickly as possible. It was to this task that they devoted their energies. Though they certainly distrusted Thiers, it never occurred to them that it was a waste of time negotiating with him, that their first duty to the Parisians was to take advantage of a military preponderance they could not long enjoy. And so, from March 18th to March 28th, ten precious days were lost.

When the Commune took over, the National Guard were

Marx said the Communards ought to have tried to make first Paris and then France socialist. He reproached them for not having plundered the Bank of France. Such bourgeois scruples, he said, were out of place in a proletarian revolution. But Marx was wrong. Had the Communards tried to force socialism on either France or Paris, they would have made nine-tenths of the French people furious without adding one battalion to their strength. Why plunder the Bank of France when they could borrow what they wanted from it? It is a pity to see Marx, usually so shrewd, arguing like a vulgar Marxist!

scarcely more effectively used than before. The Central Committee still tried to get obedience from the battalions. The Military Committee appointed by the Commune were supposed to direct military operations, but the commanders to whom they sent their orders also had to take account of the wishes of the Central Committee. The National Guard, a citizen militia, would not, unless they were greatly persuaded, leave their districts; the defence of their homes began, they thought, only a few streets away. It was not easy to move them from one part of Paris to another; it was most difficult to get them outside the capital into the open country. Some battalions of the National Guard had left Paris after the siege, but those who remained still numbered over two hundred thousand. Yet the Commune at the height of its power never had a mobile force of more than sixty thousand men. There was almost no discipline in the National Guard. It was, so the theory went, a regular and highly disciplined army that lost the Franco-Prussian war. Discipline was therefore unpopular. A revolutionary army ought to be able to do without it or with so little of it that it would hardly be noticed. The Parisians believed that the victorious armies of the first republic had been undisciplined and that their lack of discipline had not prevented them beating the Prussians. They forgot that these armies had been much more numerous than the enemy, and that they too had in the end evolved a discipline of their own, not quite the same as in other armies, but no less effective. The armies of the first republic were also willing to march anywhere. But the revolutionary élan that was supposed to take the place of discipline in the National Guard could not shift the guardsmen more than a few miles from their homes. This cult of indiscipline was perhaps the most absurd of the legacies of the first revolution. Or, rather, it was a myth invented about that revolution and not yet dispelled by the historians.

The Communards did what revolutionaries ought never to do. They waited to be attacked. They even boasted of doing so, as if their reluctance to strike hard at their enemies were a virtue. When the fighting began on April 2nd with the capture of Courbevoie by the Versaillese, the great anxiety of the Commune was to make it clear that not they but their enemies had attacked first. It is curious to see an assembly in which Jacobins and

Blanquists predominated boasting of their reluctance to make war. The Jacobins had often proved in the last thirty years that they did not always imitate what they most admired. They could bark but not bite like Robespierre. They were journalists and enthusiasts. But the Blanquists were supposed to be more serious revolutionaries. They had seldom in the past refrained from violence, even when it might have been wise to do so. They got nearer in the Commune to what they wanted than ever before, and yet they failed to take or to induce others to take the opportunities that now came their way. Some people have said that it was the absence of Blanqui that ruined the Commune. For my part, I believe he, too, would have ruined it, though in another way. He would have been aggressive and bold and might have carried the others with him; but he probably would not have understood just what was possible and what was not. He had, indeed, a terrible reputation; and yet every insurrection he organised had failed. He started his revolutionary career in 1827, and since then there had been three revolutions, each made in his absence. This is not conclusive evidence against him. Most successful revolutions are made while leading revolutionaries are away. Even Lenin had to be sent to Russia in a sealed coach after the Tsarist autocracy was destroyed. In this sphere of human activity, it has been the usual business of leaders not to start revolutions but to take control of them after they have begun. It is Blanqui's behaviour in March, April and May 1848, that makes it doubtful whether he could ever, even for a few months, have mastered a revolution after the manner of Robespierre or Lenin. He never understood what was happening in France in the early months of 1848, and he was probably no shrewder and no better informed in 1871. He would have made the Commune bolder but not less blind.

When they heard that the Versaillese had taken Courbevoie, the Communards at last decided on a single military command. They chose Cluseret, a veteran of the American civil war and an able commander. He took over on April 4th and was therefore not responsible for the disastrous failure of the Communard counter-attacks of April 3rd and 4th. Cluseret was never allowed to do what he wanted; and, above all, he was never allowed to impose discipline in the only way that seemed good to him. He was a professional soldier. He cared for his troops but did not know how to make himself popular with them; he had never been used to flatter subordinates from whom he expected obedience. In this respect he was inferior to the popular commanders, Eudes, Bergeret and Duval, who had led the Parisians to disaster just before he was made commander. Whenever Cluseret tried to impose discipline he was suspected of aiming at the dictatorship. The Communards thought they were keeping him in his place, but that place was so humble that in it he could be of no service to them. He was superseded on April 28th by another able officer, Rossel, who resigned on May 9th, exasperated by the incompetence of his superiors. He had during his short command had time to appoint brave and competent subordinates, Dombrowski, Wroblewski and La Cecilia, men better suited by temperament for revolutionary commands than either Cluseret or Rossel.

When they saw that the tide of events was moving against them, the Communards could think of no better expedient than to create a Committee of Public Safety. The Communards who belonged to the International were against it, but the others, mostly Jacobins, carried the day. The Committee of Public Safety met on May 1st and was reconstructed on May 9th, after the Versaillese had captured the fort of Issy. The Committee accomplished nothing and it nearly split the Commune. When it was reconstructed on May 9th, its members all belonged to the majority who had originally voted for its establishment and the International was no longer represented on it.[1] The minority who were opposed on principle to the Committee's existence now threatened to withdraw from the Commune. They were persuaded not to do so, but the existence of the committee still divided them from the majority. The minority were not admirers of Robespierre. A Committee of Public Safety would, they thought, destroy the democracy established by the workers of

[1] Until May 9th Gérardin, a member of the International, served on the Committee. The Blanquist, Eudes, was elected to it on May 9th. It consisted until May 9th of one member of the International and four Jacobins; after May 9th, of one Blanquist and four Jacobins. The Jacobins, extreme republicans of various kinds who belonged to no single organised body, outnumbered the Blanquists and the members of the International in the Commune by about two to one. The members of the International were in their turn almost twice as numerous as the Blanquists. These proportions are approximate.

Paris. They feared a dictatorship. What they got was just another committee, more dangerous to order than to liberty, like the ten others already in existence. If one man stood out above the others in the Committee of Public Safety, it was Delescluze. But he was a journalist and an orator, nothing more.

The Communards never fought well until after May 21st, the day when the Versaillese first penetrated into Paris. By that time they could fight once more in surroundings familiar to them, in friendly streets and behind barricades. By that time, too, military organisation had almost ceased to be important. No part of Paris is very far from any other part and the tall houses are an excellent screen. The insurgents could move quickly and unobserved from one barricade to another. Under these conditions, in spite of the large forces brought up against them, they were able to offer a fierce resistance for a week. The Versaillese troops, especially their officers, behaved with the greatest brutality. Any man or woman found with arms on his person was shot immediately. Anyone denounced as a Communard by a priest or by any other person who looked respectable was put to death without trial. During the last bloody week nearly twenty thousand persons were killed in the streets of Paris. There is nothing uglier than the vengeance of the well-to-do and respectable classes when they have been frightened by the poor.

The Communards, too, were cruel, but much less so. After the first encounters in the field, early in April, the Versaillese adopted the practice of shooting their prisoners. The Parisians, they said, had set the example. Had they not killed Generals Lecomte and Clément-Thomas? The Versaillese did not perhaps know that no one in authority in Paris had ever ordered or consented to these murders. They also thought it just to kill their prisoners because they were rebels. One of their first victims was Duval, a Communard general who was taken prisoner during the first insurgent counter-attack. The Communards had taken no prisoners. Their reply was to seize hostages in Paris and to publish a decree on April 4th threatening to put these hostages to death if the Versaillese continued to kill their prisoners. The Versaillese refused to be moved by this threat, thinking that if the Communards shot their hostages, they would do more harm to themselves than to the Versaillese, and so lend truth to Thiers' assertion that they were bandits and murderers. The Communards seem to have thought the same. Though the Versaillese killed their prisoners in greater numbers than ever, no hostages were put to death until the last week in May. The Communards then shot about a hundred persons, including one archbishop. It was all they could do in return for the thousands of their own supporters executed by the victorious Versaillese. The murder of the archbishop caused much greater indignation than the massacre of the Parisians. At that time, it was Thiers' account of the Commune that was received all over the world. Respectable people everywhere were delighted that the most terrible of French revolutions was at last suppressed; they did not learn until much later that the most terrible thing about it was the way it was suppressed.

The Commune did for republicanism in the 1870s what the June insurrection had done in the middle of the century. It discredited the socialists and the revolutionaries. But this time it did not strengthen the conservatives. They owed their predominance not to the Commune but to their pacifism. Republicanism was not injured by the defeat of red Paris. There was no Bonaparte now for the peasants to vote for. The moderate republicans had not been allies of the socialists and revolutionaries; they had not helped set up the Commune as their predecessors had helped set up the National Workshops and the Luxembourg Commission. The French people knew much more about the republicans in 1871 than in 1848. They could now make distinctions that most of them had been too ignorant to make twenty-three years ago. Most important of all, the Chief of the Executive was not a pretender aiming at absolute power; he was an old politician who had outlived his preference for monarchy and now believed that the republic would divide Frenchmen least. The monarchists were still disunited. They might, if they had acted quickly, have brought a king to France; but their own loyalties and the behaviour of the pretenders made quick action impossible. Even if they had made France a monarchy, they would have had to make her a democracy as well. The French had had manhood suffrage since 1848; and since then, first the brutality, then the weakness and at last the shameful defeat of Louis Napoleon had put them out of love with personal rule. The monarchists thought they were strong because they were the majority in the Assembly. They either did not know or chose to forget why they had been elected in February 1871. The moderate republicans, though they were the minority in the Assembly, were better interpreters of popular moods. Thiers, Ferry and Gambetta, each in his own way, spoke for a larger and more determined body of Frenchmen than any of the royalists. The moderate republicans, divided though they were on minor issues, were united in defence of the republic. Even their desire to continue the war now counted rather more in their favour than against them. The war was safely over, and it was thought a credit to France that so many of her respectable citizens had been defiant, even in defeat. It was possible to be proud of Gambetta now that he, too, had to accept the inevitable.

The failure of the Commune did no harm to the republic, but it did make the republicans more conservative than they would otherwise have been. The centre of gravity of republicanism was therefore considerably more to the right during the first decade of the third republic than during the liberal Empire. The Jacobins had had no detailed programme of social reform, but they had talked about it a great deal. If they had been powerful after 1871 and still associated with the socialists, they would soon have found it expedient to make definite promises and press for reforms. Even the less moderate of the moderates, men like Ferry and Gambetta, would have been more interested in social reform. They had often spoken of it before 1870; and if they had less to say afterwards, it was only because there was no extreme left to stimulate their interest. It was, perhaps, not a bad thing for France that the third republic was conservative for so many years before it became radical and socialist.

The Commune, like the June insurrection of 1848, for a time discredited socialism. But only for a time. When socialist groups again emerged in France, they were all the stronger and the more independent because of their memories of the Commune. In the past, in the early months of 1848 and during the Commune, the socialists had been the junior partners of the extreme republicans, the Jacobins. On both occasions they had gained little from the alliance. It had not even saved them from the bitter hostility of the moderate republicans. They had learned their lesson—or so

they thought—and they intended in future to act on their own.
The French socialists later invented the myth that the Communards failed because they were not socialist enough, or even
(and this curious theory looks more German than French)
because they did not know how socialist was the insurrection they
were making.

The Communards certainly were socialists—even many of the
Jacobins among them—in that vague and yet not unimportant
sense in which most people who say they are socialists are so.
They most of them praised socialism and meant different things
by it. But they never imagined they had taken up arms to establish
it. Anger, humiliation and contempt were the emotions that
inspired them; and all they immediately wanted was political
autonomy for Paris, the abolition of the regular army, and the
substitution for it of a citizen militia, the National Guard, in the
proletarian form it had assumed since September 1870. They
made no demands on Versailles of an even mildly socialist
character: they asked no more than that the payment of rent and
of debts should be postponed still further. Their rule in Paris was,
on the whole, respectful of property, though they did think it their
duty to see that everyone had work to do and food to eat. They
allowed the workers to run factories and workshops abandoned
by their owners, but they never confiscated any property.

The Commune was certainly a proletarian insurrection. Most
of the men elected to the municipal assembly belonged by birth to
the middle class, although there was an exceptional number of
working men among them. But though the elect were mostly
bourgeois, those who voted for them were proletarians. And at
that time the relations and sympathies binding deputies to their
constituents were exceptionally close. The Communard leaders
were perfectly aware that the movement they led was proletarian,
and they also knew that their enemies were bourgeois. They
never doubted that the struggle they were engaged in was a class
war. They had quite deliberately thrown in their lot with the
proletariat, some, no doubt, because they believed in socialism,
but most of them because they loved Paris and hated Thiers and
the Versaillese.

Chapter Seven

THE FRENCH REPUBLIC

IN 1815 there were almost no republicans in France, and in 1870 the republic was already the régime "that divides Frenchmen least." It divided them least though the next year brought civil war to France. What better proof could there be of the strength of the republicans than that they could fight this war and the republic survive it? And by republic I mean, not only absence of monarchy, but liberal democracy as well. What country in the world has known more freedom than France since 1870? What country has been more democratic?

The peculiar circumstances of the third republic's birth have given currency to a superficial judgment upon it. France became a republic, men often say, because she could not make up her mind to be anything else. They speak as if Thiers' opinion, that "the republic divides Frenchmen least," was decisive and popular, as if France accepted the republic with reluctance for lack of anything better, as if she at last became resigned to what she had never really wanted.

France, during the first years of the third republic, was tired; she had lost a foreign war and her preponderance in Europe; she had fought a civil war and at the end of it could feel relief or shame or anger but not enthusiasm. France was tired and humiliated; the coming of the republic might seem good to many, inevitable to others, and to the rest a sign of evils to come; but it was neither greatly welcomed nor greatly opposed. The republic came to a pre-occupied France, like a visitor to a house where he has been long warmly expected by some and dreaded by others, a house suddenly plunged in sorrow, so that his arrival is scarcely noticed. He finds a general indifference where he expected both affection and dislike.

When the third republic came, France was at war, and it was

still hoped that that war could be won. The change of régime was easily accepted, but no one troubled to estimate its importance; it was merely hoped that the new government would wage war more effectively than the old. When the provincials discovered that the war was lost beyond anyone's power to retrieve it—and, not being enthusiasts, they made the discovery more quickly than the Parisians and with fewer regrets—they began to resent the belligerency of the republicans. They elected royalists to the first Assembly of the new republic because the royalists promised them peace; and at that time the only important issue was whether the war should continue or be quickly brought to an end. When these elections happened, France was already a republic, and no one offered the electors a king. The candidates offered merely themselves, and most of them were peacemakers and royalists. They were elected to make peace, and, having made it, they set about deciding the political future of their country and tried to give her a king. But that the majority of Frenchmen wanted a king is most improbable; they had just lost an emperor who had been more popular with them than any of their nineteenth-century kings.

The French had, of course, supported the Versailles Assembly against the Commune; they had resisted the claim of Paris for autonomy just as they had rejected her demand for the continuance of war. But it was Thiers and his ministers, even more than the royalist Assembly, who were responsible for the victory over Paris. That victory might be described—though always with the proper qualifications—as a victory of France over Paris, or of the bourgeois and the peasants over the proletariat, or of the government at Versailles over the Commune; but it could hardly be called a victory of the royalists over the republic. It did not even help the royalists, because it did not discredit the republic. On the contrary, it strengthened it, because the victory was so complete that the provincials felt there was nothing more to be feared from the extreme radicals and revolutionaries in Paris. The republic had cut the ulcer out of herself and had made herself clean.

No one can know whether the majority of Frenchmen wanted a republic after September 1870 and in 1871; they had other more urgent problems to solve. We need not suppose that there was any majority in France decidedly in favour of, or opposed to, the republic. It may be that the royalists, had they acted quickly, could have brought a king to France, and that France might, in the end, have got used to him. But if he had come, he would have had to accept a parliamentary democracy; he would have had to make at least as many concessions to the republicans as Napoleon III made in the last years of his reign. It would not have been possible in the 1870s to revive the sort of monarchy that France knew between 1815 and 1848.

That, I think, gives us a clue to how we should interpret the dictum of Thiers that "the republic divides Frenchmen least." If we accept it as true, we must read more into it than perhaps even Thiers meant. The republic was not the régime least offensive to Frenchmen, for, indeed, it was hated by many of them. On the other hand, it was not the régime that most of them enthusiastically wanted. But more Frenchmen wanted it than any alternative; and loyalty to it was not only extensive but deep. Republicanism was already the strongest political force in France. The republicans could afford to make fewer concessions to the others than the others were obliged to make to them. We can fairly say that the royalists, even if they had been united, could never have got their king, unless they had been willing to accept everything of the republic except the name—unless they had been willing to concede almost everything that the republicans had so long fought for. What all the republicans had wanted was at last achieved in 1870; and what was not achieved was not wanted by them all.

The belief that France became a republic almost by accident, that the régime established in 1870 was provisional and only lasted because nothing was found to put in its place, that belief—though it can be excused—is certainly false. Many more Frenchmen wanted the republic in 1870 than had wanted Louis XVIII in 1815 or the Duke of Orleans in 1830; and their desire for it was stronger than their desire for Louis Napoleon's dictatorship in 1851. The republic was not a *pis aller*, something that men submitted to for the sake of peace or from indifference; it was for many a matter of faith, a system ardently longed for because to them it meant freedom, democracy and the protection of the humble against every form of privilege. It may be that a plebiscite would, for several years after September 1870, have given less votes for the republic than Napoleon III collected several times in his reign; but they would have been weightier votes, votes that represented deeper convictions and stronger loyalties. Adversity had not united the republicans; it had not made them one another's friends; but it had tried them all, and had made them politically the most combative, the most articulate and the most resolute of Frenchmen. Bonapartism had its devotees, but on the whole it was the faith of men without faith, of men indifferent to politics and afraid of responsibility, of men without positive ideas who only wanted orderly government and national glory. The Legitimists and Orleanists were small minorities; they were wealthy and had great social prestige but they were not popular. Some of them, no doubt, had a considerable following in their own localities, but taken together they stood for nothing that could attract the French people. In the eyes of most Frenchmen, probably even after Sedan, the Bonapartes were a dynasty more glorious than the Bourbons, for it had needed defeat in war, and not just a few days' rioting in Paris, to drive them out of France. From 1815 to 1848, when the Bourbons ruled, the great majority of Frenchmen were still indifferent to politics; but since that time a much greater part of the nation had been drawn into politics and the classes loyal to one or other branch of the old dynasty were no wider than before. Great skill and unity of purpose might have enabled the royalists to restore a king to the throne, but the France of after 1870 would still have been more the republicans' creation than their own. If the royalists were formidable, it was certainly not because their royalism was popular, but because they dominated the Assembly and had friends in the army and the church. Now that Bonapartism was discredited by military defeat, now that the people were silent who regretted Napoleon III much more than either Charles X or Louis Philippe had been regretted, the natural friends of authority, the high dignitaries of the church and the army, thought a restored Bourbon monarchy preferable to a republic. They wanted stability, order, and governments attentive to their interests.

Historians hostile to the republic have insisted that at the last plebiscite of the Second Empire, held in May 1870, seven and a third million people voted for the régime, and only one and a

M

half millions against it. Even in Paris the opponents of the Emperor had only a narrow majority. The Second Empire was still popular four months before its fall; when that Empire fell, the republicans seized power and ruled France in default of any-one else able to do so; and afterwards the republic continued because the royalists at first could not agree what king to put on the throne, and then, later, when at last they did agree, could not persuade him to return to France on the only acceptable terms. The republicans in Paris, according to the accounts of these historians, acted not only illegally (which no one need deny) but also as bad democrats on September 4th, 1870; they proclaimed the republic without regard for the opinions of the legislature, though that body had been freely elected only sixteen months before. The republic was first thrust upon France, and then afterwards remained with her because the people who wished to rid France of her were not united; until at last weariness, hopes deceived and habit reconciled the whole people to what only some of them had always wanted.

It is this account and the evidence it rests on, which make plausible the superficial judgment of Thiers, that "the republic divides Frenchmen least," as if the republic were a neutral and harmless thing, a dull compromise to calm the nerves of an excited people. Let us therefore examine some of this evidence. The last plebiscite of the Empire gave the régime a six to one majority; but the Empire, by that time, was already liberal; it had already conceded to the republicans a great part of what most of them wanted. These concessions were made to the republicans; they were the price paid by the Emperor either to win their sup-port or to soften their enmity. The royalists, too, wanted a more liberal régime, one that would give them opportunities they could not have under an absolute government; and they also learnt that manhood suffrage had come to stay. By making the Empire liberal, Napoleon III could not help but do what suited all his opponents; but the ones he really wished to placate, the ones whose tolerance (if not more) he must win if his dynasty were to survive, were the republicans. They had been his most formid-able opponents from December 1848, when he was elected President, until December 1851, when he made his power absolute.

At the last parliamentary elections of the Second Empire, held in May 1869, three and a third million votes were cast against the government candidates and only four and a half millions in their favour. These elections are as significant as the plebiscite held a year later. The great majority of the opposition votes were given to republicans. They were votes against authoritarian government, votes for democracy and the popular liberties, votes for all the things that the republicans, and the republicans alone, had consistently fought for for over fifty years. And when, a year later, one and a half million people voted against the Emperor, it was to show that all the concessions he had made could not win them over to him. These million and a half people were the irreconcilable enemies of the régime, who voted against it, not because it had become liberal, but because they could not trust the "Man of December" who for three years before his *coup d'état* had worked hard to destroy the very liberties he was now restoring to France. But the seven and a third millions who in May 1870 voted "yes" were not necessarily supporters of the Empire; many of them had voted against the government candidates twelve months earlier, and they had mostly voted for the republicans. By voting "yes" in May 1870 they no doubt expressed their approval of the concessions made by the Emperor; because he had made them, they accepted his dynasty, but at the time they did so there was no question of its fall. France had an Emperor who had given his country a liberal and democratic régime; it was impossible to vote for the régime without voting for the Emperor, just as it was impossible to vote for the Emperor without voting for his régime. Such is the nature of plebiscites. There was the giver and his gift; and the French people had to say "yes" or "no" to both of them.

I do not mean to suggest that the persons who voted against the government in May 1869 and for the liberal Empire in May 1870 wanted to be rid of the Emperor though they accepted his gift, that they voted "yes" at the plebiscite because they liked the gift more than they disliked the giver. No doubt, many of them were quite reconciled to the dynasty by the Emperor's concessions; and no doubt, too, others who had voted against his government in May 1869 had never wanted a republic. But they had wanted much that the republicans asked for, and had wanted it enough to resist the considerable pressure that the authorities were still able to put on the electors in 1869. The republic was ardently desired by a formidable minority, a minority more formidable than any other opposed to the régime; and what the republicans stood for—democracy, liberty, and even (though this more vaguely) social reform—was desired by a minority so large that it was no longer possible to rule France against their wishes. These are, I think, the reasonable conclusions to be drawn from the elections of 1869 and the plebiscite of 1870. The liberal Empire had an excellent chance of survival; it was destroyed by the folly of its government and the unscrupulous cleverness of Bismarck. It was certainly the most popular régime France had had since the end of the first Empire. But it does not follow that the third republic, when it came, was not also (though, no doubt, quite differently) popular. It had fewer lukewarm and more zealous friends than the Empire, and it had as many and as bitter enemies. If, then, the republic divided Frenchmen least, it was certainly not because most of them were indifferent to it; it was because, now that the Bonapartists were disgraced, there was no alternative régime nearly as popular, and also because the republicans were more formidable and more pugnacious than they had ever been. It was the advantage of the royalists—their predominance in the Assembly—that was temporary and fortuitous; if they did not quickly give France a parliamentary and democratic monarchy they could give her no monarchy at all. For a short time they had a slender chance, and they failed to take it.

The historians who underestimate the strength of the republicans in the early seventies forget two things: the nature of the opposition to the Empire, and the history of the second republic. Charles X and Louis Philippe had never had to bear such attacks as were made on Napoleon III during the last years of his reign; the republicans had never been so numerous, so conscious of their strength, and so contemptuous of their enemies; Paris had never before taken such liberties with a ruler of France. The Emperor had felt his weakness, and his concessions had proved that the hostility of the republicans frightened him more than his plebiscites and parliamentary majorities could reassure him. He had, while President of the Republic, intrigued his way to power, had taken a few risks and had used force; but towards the end of his reign, illness and frustration made him nervous, hesitant and weak. His instinct was to placate the strong, to make his rule and his dynasty tolerable to the men who would otherwise, perhaps later, perhaps sooner, destroy them. He knew that the republicans were much stronger in the 1860s than they had been just before the fall of the July Monarchy. The revolutions of 1830 and 1848 were victories of the weak over the faint-hearted; and since then the political struggle had grown wider and more intense.

It was the republicans who widened it and made it more intense; and it was the second republic which gave them their opportunity. The February revolution had been a surprise to most Frenchmen; they had grown tired of Guizot and his clever and tedious king, but they had not thought of using force against them. The July Monarchy had been useful to some, contemptible to others, and indifferent to most; and it had been almost without wanting it that the republicans had frightened the king out of France. Once the king had gone, they could not help congratulating themselves on their success; and, of course, they never doubted their fitness to govern. The country accepted them because they had presented themselves at an opportune moment, because they were new, hopeful and interesting, because they had recently behaved well and had frightened nobody. At the first elections after the February revolution the French voted in their millions for the republic; they were pleased to have the vote and they chose the men of the hour. France was never, politically, in a better humour than for a few months after she was rid of Guizot and the Orleanist king. But because she gave the republic a warm welcome, she was not therefore republican. The republicans were on trial, and it would need only a few mistakes to dissipate all the good will France felt for them. Those mistakes the republicans made with an alacrity that even their enemies had not expected, and from the June days onward the progress of reaction was slow but sure. That much all the world could see. But what was less easily seen was the progress of the republicans. Two abortive acts of violence, the Blanquist invasion of the Assembly on May 15th and the June insurrection, had frightened all France, but they had also destroyed or at least silenced the revolutionary wing of the republican movement. For three and a half years the republicans were on the defensive, and they could only defend themselves and the republic by trying to make converts among the people. For three and a half years they made such propaganda as no one else in France was interested in making. They could not rely, like the conservative royalists of the Party of Order, on the wealthy and the privileged; nor could they rely, like the Prince-President, on a great name and on the army and the police. They could rely only on the people, but they had first to win them over to their cause. The conservatives quite naturally ignored or distrusted the people; they did not believe in democracy, for they had been powerful when the electorate was narrow. Louis Napoleon did not ignore the people, and he despised rather than distrusted them; he flattered them, made promises to them and took account of their prejudices. He wished to be popular, but had no faith in the people and no ambitions for them. But the republicans had a faith they wished the people to share; they were zealots and missionaries; they wanted not the people's indifference, nor their blind loyalty, nor their passive benevolence, but their active collaboration in a great cause. They were the apostles of liberty, equality and fraternity, words that cynics called empty, though the people could translate them in a thousand ways to suit their needs and prejudices. Seventy years of the third republic have robbed these words of their magic, but to the republicans of 1848–51, fighting a long battle against a conservative Assembly and a President who wanted to destroy the republic he was elected to preside over, they were a message of hope worth great sacrifices. Republicanism was then something unique in French politics, something younger, bolder, more hopeful and more dangerous than the forces it opposed. It was an appeal to the people to take politics seriously for the sake of justice and in their own interest; it was an appeal to their hearts and their minds, requiring courage and intelligence of them. The republicans were active in the towns and in many of the country districts, and wherever they went they created an interest in politics among classes that had not known it before. By December 2nd, 1851, they had won over to their cause a minority of the people, but it was a much larger minority than had supported it before February 1848. For the political education, good or bad, of the French people during the nineteenth century, the republicans were more responsible than all the other parties put together. It was natural that it should be so, for they alone had faith in the people and therefore spoke to them as no one else could. Several generations of republican activity prepared the coming of the third republic. It needed a greater effort to make France a republic than to make her a monarchy, Bourbon or Bonapartist. Why, then, should we be astonished that the republic, when at last it came, should have stayed so long?

*   *   *   *   *

But the republican movement was also revolutionary in a sense that I have several times tried to explain. Only a small part of it deliberately used violence as a political method, but the ideals common to the whole movement were inherited from the great revolution—and more particularly from the Girondins and Jacobins of the Convention. Moreover, in their pursuit of these ideals, the republicans—even the most moderate of them—were for fifty years an illegal opposition. Whether they liked it or not, the nature of the régimes they opposed forced them into activities that brought revolutions to France, and when those revolutions happened, they quite naturally took over the government. Though most of them did not deliberately make revolutions, they all profited from them. To their enemies they all looked like revolutionaries of whom only some had the courage of their convictions. They praised the great revolution, they excused the later and smaller ones, they made heroes of the Girondins and Montagnards, and the enemies of the first republic were also their enemies.

On the left wing of the republican movement there soon arose socialism, the natural consequence of applying republican principles to the economic as well as the political sphere. And French socialism—because it made its first working-class converts in Paris, the city of revolution—was inevitably in part revolutionary. It was, of course, reformist as well; and all the early leaders of French socialism—the disciples of Saint-Simon, Fourier, Cabet and Louis Blanc—were men of peace. But it was inevitable, in the peculiar atmosphere of Paris, that socialism should also become revolutionary. It was the workers who fought on the barricades, and it was the workers who were most attracted to socialism; so that, not only did socialism become in part revolutionary, but the revolutionary wing of the republican movement became socialist. And as it became socialist, it drew away from the moderates, found it more difficult to work with them, frightened and exasperated them, and at last took up arms against them.

The Marxists explain this quite simply. They say that at first the workers were the instruments of the bourgeois; they did the fighting and the bourgeois won the victories. During the great revolution the workers were the tools of the Jacobins, and in 1830 they were the dupes of the liberals; but in 1848, and still more in 1871, they shook free of the bourgeois and tried to make their own terms with society. And for this show of independence they were twice dreadfully punished, in June 1848 and in May 1871.

This explanation is not implausible. The moderate republicans, who were the great majority, did resent what they considered the truculent socialism of the Paris workers; they exaggerated the extent of their demands on society and were afraid of the reactions of the provinces. They wanted to turn what they called "socialism" into harmless channels, to dissipate its strength, and at last, when they were really frightened, to destroy it. But what most frightened them was the violence of the revolutionaries; and, to do them justice, they were more anxious for the popularity of the republican cause in France than for their own class interests. Where there is no theory to blind us to the facts, they seem obvious enough. The moderate republican leaders did not really believe that the revolutionaries in Paris could destroy, or ever seriously threaten, the institution of property; but they certainly believed that their "extravagance" would turn the country against the republic. It was their interest of course to appear to the people as defenders of property; just as it was the interest of the conservatives to pretend that all republicans were either enemies of property or else—because every revolutionary movement is at the mercy of its extremists—were incapable of properly defending it. There was much excited talk about property in 1848, but no real threat to it and no need to defend it.

The great fault of the moderate republicans was that they did not know how small and cheap were the concessions that would have satisfied the workers in 1848. They mistook the nature of the National Workshops, and quite wrongly attributed a socialist character to them. Had they taken better care of the workers, had they understood their needs, they could have weakened the revolutionaries without shedding a drop of blood, and so have prevented them frightening the great passive majority of the nation.

We are still greatly misled by the Marxists. Not that they have been more foolish or more wrong than other people, not that their myths are the least closely related to reality. On the contrary, they have often been shrewd and still more often plausible; and there is about their theories a certain air of authority that only familiarity can dissipate. They have accustomed us, even when we are not Marxists, to explain political movements in terms of class interests. The bourgeois, we say, are people so placed in society, and therefore have definite interests of their own and elaborate a political and social philosophy that suits those interests; and the same is true, with all the appropriate differences, of the other classes. It is not necessary, if you reject this theory, to deny either that classes have interests or that politics is largely concerned with conflicts between those classes. It is also concerned with other things, but that is not what I now want to discuss. My point is merely that it does not follow that, because classes have interests and politics is largely concerned with conflicts between classes, what those classes quarrel about is chiefly their interests or else something "ideological" determined by those interests. Nor does it follow that the classes quarrel because their interests are irreconcilable. It is much more difficult to reconcile men than interests; and it is the more difficult the more they have quarrelled. Besides, men have no interests prior to their conceptions of justice. They are made moral by the same process that makes them social, and their interests are those things which they think it right they should have and which they strive to obtain. Their needs or interests are as much determined by their ideals as they determine them, and to presume either prior to the other is to make the cardinal and simple error destructive of all clear thinking about politics. The Marxists are not the only people who have foisted this error upon us, but their present importance makes it appear peculiarly their own.

We must not believe that the moderate republicans and the socialists quarrelled because they spoke for different classes whose interests were irreconcilable. Do we even know what is meant by "irreconcilable" interests? What limits are there to the agreements men can make, to their concessions and sacrifices? They sometimes astonish themselves by their generosity, and at other times they astonish their friends by their meanness. What reason have we to believe that classes are more consistent than individuals? What seems impossible at one time seems easy at another. Men and groups of men will always quarrel, and yet it will never be true that they are in principle irreconcilable. If the moderates and the socialists quarrelled in 1848 and again in 1871, it was certainly not because the bourgeois and the workers had irreconcilable interests. They quarrelled for reasons that political theory cannot guess at, reasons that only the historian can discover.

But they did quarrel, and their quarrels greatly affected the history of France. They made republicanism appear more dangerous, and strengthened all its opponents; they weakened the sympathies of the bourgeois republicans for the workers, and they made the workers angry and suspicious of the bourgeois; they made the "class war" look more real than any divergence of economic interests could have done. The moderate republicans, after all, were not rich; they were not bankers and industrialists, but mostly professional men, lawyers and journalists, men who had nothing to lose if the workers prospered. The success of the National Workshops would not have injured them; nor, indeed, would it have injured the bankers and manufacturers; it would have done no harm to anybody and would have prevented the June insurrection and massacre. The workers no more wanted to destroy property than the moderates needed to defend it; many of them had heard of socialism and had liked what they heard, and some of them had even understood it; but their actual demands were always modest. They wanted security and a living wage; and nobody would have been the worse off if they had got them. But the moderates had illusions about the workers, who also had illusions about them; and therefore they quarrelled. No doubt, they would never have quarrelled as bitterly as they did, they would never have acquired their pernicious illusions, had they not belonged to different classes, unaccustomed to understand one another. They wanted different things, and they wanted them so much that they came to blows; but the things they so desperately wanted were not always the same; they changed with the times and were never the means to any permanent interests irreconcilable with the interests of other classes. The things they wanted so much that they were ready to fight for them were themselves the products of their illusions. The June days and the Commune of 1871 were the two most terrible class conflicts of the nineteenth century, but neither of them happened through the permanent interests of the combatants being irreconcilable. Their causes I have tried to describe in the course of this book, and there is no need now to repeat the description.

These two battles have had an unfortunate effect on French politics. They have increased the hostility between classes, and have strengthened the belief that conflict between them is inevitable. The interests of the social classes have been as different in England as in France, but the conflicts of classes have been less bitter. Marx noticed the peculiar bitterness of these conflicts in France, and set it down to the realism and political maturity of the French proletariat. I have no wish to quarrel with compliments paid to the French. They are brave, intelligent and resolute; and they are also as well aware of their interests as most people. But it is not to these qualities that they owe their revolutionary history. Their first and greatest revolution was unpremeditated, and it made such vast changes in their country that they could never forget it. It created in some a horror of revolution, and in others a cult of it. It bred enthusiasms, suspicions and fears, and so made politics more dangerous and exciting; it gave a sharper edge to ambition and made class loyalties more intense; but it did nothing to improve men's understanding of society and of their own permanent interests inside it.

The republican and socialist movement, in spite of the anxieties and hesitations of the majority at every approach of danger (hesitations as much due to fears for France as for themselves), was always, in a special and important sense, revolutionary. Perhaps it could not be otherwise. The collapse of the old society and the political inexperience of the French allowed the extremists to get control of the country within a few years of the meeting of the States-General. This victory of the extremists was never repeated, because in all the later revolutions fear of the extreme left was stronger than fear of reaction. The moderates, as soon as a revolution happened, quickly forgot the enemies to the right of them for fear of their late allies turned enemies to the left. Within a few months or weeks of a successful revolution, the distribution of forces changed. These changes were the effects of the competitive struggle for power. Since revolutions were made in Paris (and where else could they be made in a highly centralised state?), their first effect was to strengthen the extremists against the moderates. The moderates were therefore inevitably placed in the position of the Girondins; they defended the rights of France against the excessive zeal of the extremists in Paris. As soon as an Assembly was freely elected by the people, they defended it against the Parisians. It was their misfortune in 1848 that all the republicans were blamed by the provincials for the violence of the "reds" in Paris; and it was their better fortune in 1871 and the years following that France had learnt to make distinctions she had not made twenty-three years before. But what the various groups were fighting for in 1830, in 1848-51 and in 1870-1, was power; what they intended to do with it when they got it was not made clear to anyone. Did the leaders themselves know? They declared principles and repeated slogans but they made no precise promises. How, indeed, could they have done so? Only the "reactionaries" had experience of government, and they were interested in preventing change. The republicans had no such experience, and they knew nothing of the problems that must face them as soon as they began to govern. It was their interest to create as many hopes and as few fears as possible, and therefore to be general and vague. Even the leaders on the extreme left hand had no "programme" of the kind that British electors, for instance, have been taught to expect from the major parties competing for their votes. They had only their principles and their aspirations; and when they made demands that were more precise, they were always modest. The greatest threat to property ever made by the revolutionaries was the demand for a progressive income tax.

We must always distinguish between men's dreams and the actual demands they make on society. There were Frenchmen who had visions of a communist society, and who believed in its eventual coming; there were anarchists and socialists of many different kinds. The Blanquists even believed in the violent destruction of the old society. But these aspirations and beliefs, though they affected men's actions, did not therefore constitute threats to society. The Blanquists could not act alone; they had to make alliances and therefore compromises; they could not ask for more than their allies were willing to fight for. The most extreme demands of the Paris Commune were political; they were a threat to the unity of France much more than to the institution of property. Even revolutionaries are to some extent realists; they have some idea of the most that they can, under the circumstances, get away with. The Communards thought they might get a large measure of self-government for Paris, but even the socialists in the Commune knew that property was an institution too firmly established to be touched by them.

Of course, the various groups competing for power had their clients in different classes; and their principles and slogans, as well as their more precise demands, were adapted to the needs and prejudices of those classes. The leaders either belonged by birth to those classes or else were drawn to them by sympathy; they were interested in them and were anxious to make life easier and more secure for them, though they had often only the vaguest idea how this should be done. But their slogans and precise demands were as much (and indeed more) determined by the course of the political struggle, by memories of past victories and defeats, by popular reactions to particular events, as by anything that could fairly be called "class interests." If the political struggle was violent it was certainly not because the clash of these interests required it should be so; for the poor have extorted far greater concessions from the rich since 1871 than before it. And the reason they have done so is obvious enough: France has been a parliamentary democracy for eighty years (excepting the years stolen by Hitler); the workers have been represented in parliament by able advocates, who have made precise demands on their behalf, have produced arguments difficult to refute, and have been listened to even by the advocates of the rich. Justice is now the name for many things that would have been called robbery less than a century ago.

Not that the republicans were more to blame than their opponents for the series of revolutions that have so much divided Frenchmen. Revolutions happen not because there are, "below the level of politics," inevitable and irremediable social incompatibilities, but because those who govern are, for reasons peculiar to their time and place, no longer able or willing to find the remedies. It is not in the nature of the social phenomena called "incompatible" that there should be no means of adjusting them to one another peacefully; it is merely that men, for reasons that are discoverable but not always the same, do not look for, or do not find, what will enable them to avoid violence. Put aside political conflicts and the way they are conducted, look only at their social causes, and you will never discover a reason why they should not be peaceably settled. If the republican and socialist movement never lost its revolutionary character it was because the successive governments of France did not sufficiently attend to the grievances which made that movement possible. On the other hand, the blindness and obduracy of these governments were themselves partly the effects of their constant fear of disorder. The revolutionaries threatened too much and the governments conceded too little. Both attitudes were excusable, since each was a natural reaction to the other. The governments forgot that in a country like France, a country transformed by one of the two greatest revolutions of modern times (a revolution which had enabled an extreme minority to gain power and to exercise it ruthlessly for fourteen months), demands for reform will be pressed less patiently and respectfully, with greater truculence and more threats than across the Channel. Memories of successful violence make violence, verbal and physical, easier. As for the republicans, they forgot that their methods made it more difficult rather than easier for governments to concede their demands. They frightened and therefore could not persuade. It is true that their enemies were sometimes so frightened that they ran out of France, but the republicans then found themselves too weak and too divided to govern. They frightened the bourgeois and peasants; they frightened each other; and they never decided, distracted as they were by the fears, suspicions and intrigues engendered by their quarrels, just what it was they wanted to do, either for France or for the humbler classes who supported them.

Let no one be in a hurry to condemn either their folly or their motives. They were the victims, as well as the heirs, of the great revolution; they were in opposition almost continually for over fifty years; they were never united in one body, they never knew their strength or their weakness, nor could ever calculate the effect of their own actions. They were not even prepared for the revolutions whose immediate causes were their own actions. These disabilities were imposed upon them by circumstances, by the darkness or half-light they worked in, by their long experience of opposition and short experience of power, by the illiteracy and anger of some of their more active supporters, and by memories of violence and oppression. And yet they were, all told, more humane, these republicans and revolutionaries of the nineteenth century, than the Girondins and Montagnards of 1792–94; they were most of them men of principle, honest, generous and patriotic. Nor were they stupid. The government of France, whenever they took it over, was never a going concern; they had no loyal and impartial departments of state ready to serve them, and no instrument like the English parliament, with strength and dignity enough to impose certain standards of behaviour on all its members, however trivial and foolish nature may have made them.

The conservatives, too, were victims of the great revolution, but in another sense. They were not now its victims as they had been from 1792–94; they were never defeated by the extremists in the nineteenth century. On the contrary, they recovered power with remarkable ease only a few months after February 1848, and they had a greater share of it than the moderate republicans for several years after 1871. But they feared the "reds" too much, and made them only the more dangerous by refusing to make timely concessions to the workers of Paris. In May and June 1848 they did their best to excite the moderates against the Jacobins and socialists, and in March 1871, though they could easily have calmed them, they defied the Parisians to do their worst. Their fear of the revolutionaries blinded them; they imagined their world on the edge of disaster and could feel for nobody except themselves. And fear is an even worse counsellor than anger, for it robs men of the two qualities by which they are most essentially human: charity and self-respect.[1]

It was no incompatibility of permanent interests which made the republicans enemies of the church. This enmity too, was a legacy of the great revolution. It is true that the philosophers who formed the minds of the first revolutionaries were hostile either to religion or to the church. But neither they nor their disciples wanted to destroy the church; they wanted no more than to curtail her privileges and her influence, to allow men to live without her, and without her interference, should they feel so inclined. The lower clergy, and they were the majority, supported the first revolution during its earlier phases; they turned against it (taking the faithful with them) only after the state had presumed to impose a constitution on the church. The state need never have imposed it, and would not have made the attempt, had it not first, to save itself from bankruptcy, deprived the church of her estates. Having made the church financially dependent on itself, the state decided it had a right and a duty to interfere with the organisation of the church. The revolutionaries who first interfered soon learnt their mistake, and they tolerated a disobedience which their own interference had made necessary. But when more extreme revolutionaries succeeded them, the church was persecuted; and the republic, which so greatly altered that church, became her enemy. The memory of this persecution stood between the republicans and the church all through the nineteenth century; it opposed to each other the two most popular loyalties in France. The church (and later the conservatives) came to believe that only schools controlled by herself could preserve France against doctrines subversive of society and religion; and the republicans were as certain that the republic could never be firmly established while so many of the laity were educated in church schools. They were both wrong; or, rather, they were

[1] But they were not victims, like the moderate men in the Convention, of the worst fear of all, which robs men of their wills. M. Léon Blum, describing his impressions of Vichy in July, 1940, said: "Ce qui agissait, c'était la peur . . . Ce qu'on appelait le Marais dans les assemblées révolutionnaires a connu une peur de ce genre le 31 mai ou le 9 thermidor. J'ai compris, je vous assure, pourquoi on avait appelé cela le Marais. C'était vraiment un marécage humain, dans lequel on voyait, je le repète, à vue d'œil, se dissoudre, se corroder, disparaître tout ce qu'on avait connu à certains hommes de courage et de droiture."—L. Blum to the High Court of Justice, July 27th, 1945. Quoted by Zévaès, *Histoire de la Troisième République*, pp. 343–4.

partly right because they were mostly wrong. Because they believed that schools might be used to preach doctrines destructive of what they most esteemed, both the church and the republicans used their schools against their opponents.

*   *   *   *   *

We have been told so often, that we are in danger of believing it, that the different classes acquire incompatible ideologies suitable to their irreconcilable interests. The man who did most to make this belief popular was a student of French history; he wrote two long pamphlets about the second republic and another about the Commune. Karl Marx, the revolutionary socialist, took a special interest in the country of revolutions. And yet there is no better evidence against this, one of his most cherished beliefs, than the history of the revolutionary movement in France. French socialism was the child of republicanism; it was a simple extension to the social sphere of the political doctrines of the eighteenth-century philosophers and bourgeois revolutionaries. These political doctrines were in no way exclusive of socialism; and it soon occurred to men that they could not be applied until the poor, the great majority of the people, were made fit for democracy, that political equality could not exist until social inequalities were greatly diminished. But how could they be diminished? Must the state intervene to diminish them? Even Robespierre and the Mountain, though they proclaimed the sanctity of property, gave an affirmative answer to this last question. They were not socialists but they were friends of the poor; and the difference between what they were willing to do for the poor and the prescriptions of the later socialists was more a difference of method than of aim. Socialism came to France before there was a demand for it by the class in whose interest it was invented; nor was it a theory produced for their benefit independently of bourgeois "ideology." It was the natural issue, born in bourgeois minds, of that ideology; and the workers took to it (or to as much of it as they could understand) because they had first accepted the principles of 1789, because they had learnt that the "rights of man" were meant as much for them as for other people. Proudhon was right when he said that the justice preached by the philosophers and revolutionaries of the eight-

N

eenth century implies social equality and therefore the transformation of the existing order; he had a more intimate knowledge than Marx of French revolutions and of the workers in
Paris; and he also knew that every theory has its ancestry of
ideas, and therefore a considerable independence of prevailing
social conditions.

The revolutionaries of France were never united and they were
the devotees, more or less enlightened, of many different creeds.
But there were two men, Rousseau and Proudhon, who, more
than the others, formed their minds. Not that the revolutionaries
ever attempted, in sober seriousness, to re-create society in the
image of their utopias. But it was from them they learned to
distrust all governments not closely responsible to the people, to
consider the wealth of the few incompatible with the independence of the many, and to believe that justice is impossible without
equality and equality without freedom.

A SELECT BIBLIOGRAPHY

I. GENERAL

A. AULARD. *Histoire Politique de la Révolution Française.*
A. MATHIEZ. *La Révolution Française.*
J. PASTRE. *Histoire de la Restauration.*
P. M. THUREAU-DANGIN. *Histoire de la Monarchie de Juillet.*
P. DE LA GORCE. *Histoire du Second Empire.*
E. LAVISSE (ed.). *Histoire de la France Contemporaine* (Vols. IV–VII).
(S. Charléty, in Vols. IV and V, covers the period 1815 to 1848, and
C. Seignobos, in Vols. VI and VII, the period 1848 to 1875).
J. CLAPHAM. *Economic Development of France and Germany* (1815–1914).

II. REPUBLICANISM

L. BLANC. *Histoire de Dix Ans.*
G. WEILL. *Histoire du Parti Républicain en France.*
J. TCHERNOFF. *Le Parti Républicain sous la Monarchie de Juillet.*
Associations et Sociétés Secrètes sous la Deuxième République.
Le Parti Républicain au Coup d'État et sous le Second Empire.

III. SOCIALISM AND THE WORKING CLASS

A. LICHTENBERGER. *Le Socialisme et la Révolution Française.*
E. LAVASSEUR. *Histoire des Classes Ouvrières et de l'Industrie en France de 1789 à 1870.*
E. DOLLÉANS. *Histoire du Mouvement Ouvrièr* (Vol. I).
P. LOUIS. *Histoire du Socialisme en France depuis la Révolution iusqu'à nos Jours.*
S. CHARLÉTY. *Saint-Simon et les Saint-Simoniens.*
G. WEILL. *L'École Saint-Simonienne.*
A. LICHTENBERGER. *Le Socialisme Utopique.*
E. DOLLÉANS. *Proudhon.*
G. WEILL. *Histoire du Mouvement Social en France* (1852–1900).
M. DOMMANGET. *Blanqui.*

IV. CHURCH AND STATE

A. DEBIDOUR. *Histoire des Rapports de l'Église et de l'État en France* (1789–1870).
E. DE PRESSENSÉ. *L'Église et la Révolution Française.*
G. WEILL. *Histoire du Catholicisme Libéral en France* (1828–1908).
Histoire de l'Enseignement Secondaire en France.
Histoire de l'Idée Laïque en France au XIX Siècle.
J. MAURAIN. *La Politique Ecclésiastique du Second Empire* (1852–69).
E. LECANUET. *Montalembert.*

v. THE REVOLUTIONS OF THE NINETEENTH CENTURY

E. L. WOODWARD. *French Revolutions.*

F. GUIZOT. *Mémoires pour Servir à l'Histoire de Mon Temps* (Vol. I).

L. BLANC. *Histoire de Dix Ans* (Vol I).

A. FABRE. *La Révolution de 1830 et le Véritable Parti Républicain.*

A. CRÉMIEUX. *La Révolution de Février 1848.*

A. DE LAMARTINE. *Histoire de la Révolution de 1848.*

J. JAURÈS (ed.). *Histoire Socialiste* (Vol. IX).

E. THOMAS. *Histoire des Ateliers Nationaux.*

D. MACKAY. *The National Workshops (A Study in the French Revolution of 1848).*

F. SIMPSON. *The Rise of Louis Napoleon.*

K. MARX. *The Eighteenth Brumaire of Louis Bonaparte.*

E. MASON. *The Paris Commune.*

J. JAURÈS (ed.). *Histoire Socialiste* (Vol. XI).

P. DOMINIQUE. *La Commune.*

G. DA COSTA. *La Commune Vécue.*

INDEX

Agoult, Mme d', 116
Aide-toi, le Ciel t'aidera, 37, 39, 51
Albert, 67, 112
Amis du Peuple, Les (see The Friends of
the poeple)
Ariège, Arnaud de l', 146
Assignats, The, 8-9
Association for the Liberty of the Press,
The, 39, 51
Avant-Garde, L', 63
Avenir, L', 49
Audriffet-Pasquier, Duc d', 126
August 10th, 1792, Insurrection of, 4,
10-12, 18
Aurelle de Paladines, General d', 139

Babeuf, F-E (Gracchus), 17, 27, 45
Banquet Campaign, The, 61-3
Barbès, Armand, 46, 56, 62, 70, 76, 78
Barrot, Odilon, 65, 67, 83, 91, 98
Bazaine, Marshal, 134
Bazard, Armand, 22-3, 25-6, 42
Bergeret, 153
Bernard, Martin, 46
Bismarck, Prince Otto von, 135, 142,
164
Blanc, Louis: Marx's opinion of, x;
influence during July Monarchy, 26,
42-4, 47, 62, 89; joins Provisional
Government, 67; influence and behaviour during the Second Republic,
71-2, 78, 82; exile in London, 112;
refusal of amnesty, 114, 122; dislike
of violence, 167
Blanqui, Auguste: his first insurrection,
27; his attitude to revolution, 45-6;
leading member of the Amis du
Peuple, 52; makes insurrection of
May 1837, 56; imprisonment, 62;
behaviour immediately after the
February 1848 revolution, 69-70;
distrusted by Ledru-Rollin, 74; his
part in insurrection of May 15th 1848,
76, 79; renewed imprisonment, 78,
112; influence on workers during
Second Republic, 89-90; activities

during Second Empire, 122; attacks
Government of National Defence,
134; sentenced to death in absentia,
139; estimate of B. as revolutionary
leader, 152
Blum, Léon, 176 *n.*
Bonaparte (see Napoleon I)
Bonaparte, Louis (see Napoleon III)
Boulevard des Capucines Fusillade, The,
65, 69
Broglie, Albert, duc de, 126
Bugeaud, Marshal, 65-6
Buonarotti, Filippo, 27, 45
Buzenval, Sortie towards, 135

Cabet, Étienne, 26, 42-3, 56, 70, 89, 167
Carrel, Armand, 55
Caussidière, Marc, 70, 76
Cavaignac, Eugène, 79, 83
Cavaignac, Godefroy, 41
Central Committee of the National
Guard, The, 140, 142-6, 148, 150-1
Central Committee of the Twenty Dis-
tricts, The, 133-5
Chambord, Comte de, 98-9
Chambrées, Les, 117
Changarnier, General, 99-100
La Charbonnerie, 23-7
Charles X, King, 1, 22, 29-37, 51, 107,
109, 110, 161, 164
Chartists, The English, 51, 53
Châtiments, Les, 113
Chevaliers de la Liberté, Les, 24
Civil Constitution of the Clergy, The, 6
Clémenceau, Georges, 115-16, 122, 144,
146
Clément-Thomas, General, 142, 154
Club de la Révolution, Le, 70
Club des Amis du Peuple, Le, 70
Cluseret, 152-3
Collège Ste-Barbe, Le, 116
Combat, Le, 134-5
Committee of Public Safety, The, 16
Commune, The (first), 3-5, 10-14, 16,
40
Commune of 1871, The, *passim*